PHUKET, LET'S GOLF

Twelve Guys, One week, Zero Self Control

Written by

Simon Mennell

Copyright

Disclaimer

This book is a work of fiction. Names, characters, businesses, places, events, and incidents are either the products of the author's imagination or used in a fictitious manner. Any resemblance to actual persons, living or dead, or actual events is purely coincidental.

The views and opinions expressed in this book are those of the characters and do not necessarily reflect the views or opinions of the author or the publisher. This book is intended purely for entertainment purposes, and the author and publisher assume no responsibility for any actions taken as a result of reading this fiction.

Dedication

To the boys, you know who you are.

And to Krapow, my silent co-author, paid exclusively in
doggy treats

Contents

Chapter One

When Hope Smells Like Wet Grass

Steam rolled across the bathroom mirror like smoke on a battlefield. Bruce stood beneath the shower, letting the hot water thump against his shoulders, trying to loosen the stiffness in his neck—and the years in his bones.

From the bathroom, through the open door, the old bedside radio crackled into life as the DJ announced.

"Alright folks, you're tuned into Punk Power Hour, diving deep into the golden age of British punk. Next up — Raise the Roof Tonight by York's very own local legends, The Shove. Loud, proud and ugly enough to wake the dead. They were responsible for a crowd-pleasing terrace anthem for York City fans. I wonder where they are now, probably stuck behind the tills at the local petrol station, no doubt." Chuckling as the music came to life. Then came the squall of guitars, all raw energy and glorious imperfection. It hit like a boot through a pub door—fast, chaotic, and full of bite.

Bruce grinned as the chorus kicked in. "Ah, the soundtrack of our youth," he muttered, turning off the tap and reaching for the towel. "Back when we thought shouting in a band meant you were cool." He paused. A quiet moment hung in the steam. Where the hell have all those years gone? In the blink of an eye, gigs had turned into garden centres. Pints into pills. Festivals into funerals. And now, here he was—pushing sixty, and weekend golf games in pouring rain.

He padded through to the bedroom, towel slung low, and wiped a clear patch in the misted-up mirror. Staring back at him: greying stubble, lines etched deep around the eyes, and hair retreating like it owed someone money. A face softened by laughter, hardened by life. It looked tired—but still had fight in it.

He squinted, straightened up, and gave himself a nod. "Good morning, Brucie – you handsome bugger." Then came the ritual.

On went the crimson golf polo—the one that clung slightly around the middle but made him feel like he meant business. Lightweight chinos, bright white ankle socks, golf trainers that hadn't seen polish in years, and a spritz of aftershave with a name that sounded vaguely Italian but came from a petrol station. He zipped up his waterproof jacket, grabbed his holdall, and took one final glance around the room. It was time.

As he drove down the street, the sky was an endless sheet of dull dark clouds, it's the kind of weather where even the sheep look properly pissed off. Raindrops pelted the roof and windshield with a relentless, insistent rhythm, as if the sky itself was angry. The wipers squeaked rhythmically, attempting to clear the streaks of water, but the glass remained streaked, wayward lines of moisture that blurred the world outside. The thick smell of damp earth and wet concrete seeped into the car, mingling with the crisp scent of rain on cold metal.

Bruce shook his head, and made a deep sigh as the car moved slowly along the deserted street, headlights slicing through the heavy gloom. He pulled up outside John's house and sat silently, clasping the steering wheel tightly, eyes fixed ahead. The early light was struggling to pierce the thick clouds—just a dull, washed-out glow—hardly enough to lift the mood. A cold wind shook the trees, leaves swirling in lazy circles across the driveway, indifferent to the rain.

He watched as John sat at the kitchen table, staring out at the storm. His face reflected a mixture of resignation and casual acceptance—almost like he was used to mornings like this. A steaming mug of coffee sat beside him, a lazy swirl of steam curling upward, but the thick slice of heavily buttered toast still on his plate remained untouched. The scene looked frozen in time, a slice of life in the drizzly grey.

"You're bloody mad going out in this to play golf. You need your head read!" his wife Sandra said, wrapped in her dressing gown and shaking her head. John grabbed the toast in his hand, pecked Sandra on the cheek and walked out of the kitchen. A moment later, the front door swung open. John appeared, wrapped up in thick waterproofs, as tight as a strait jacket, and a cup of coffee in hand, and clubs over his back. Just as he stepped outside, his wife, standing in the doorway in her dressing gown, called out with mock exasperation. "You're all bloody crazy!"

John looked over, giving her a lopsided smile as he slipped into the car and shouted back. "It's March—could be worse, could be snowing" he said with laughter and winked at her, then shut the car door with a thud.

Bruce chuckled as he shifted into gear. "You're not wrong, mate" he said, pulling away from the curb. "All this rain, and you're still in good spirits. I can't stand it, but I admire your dedication"

John shook his head with a grin. "Someone's got to keep the optimism alive, right? Though I'd rather be inside, cozy, Sandra looking provocative in her wool dressing gown, and with a proper coffee."

Bruce burst out laughing. "In your dreams brother, in your bleeding dreams".

Then turned onto the main road, glancing over at his friend. "Well, you're here now, no time for romance, and I've got a feeling we're in for one hell of a soggy round. Least it's early, so the course will be empty—perfect for losing a few balls in the mud."

There was a brief silence as the rain started to patter against the windshield again, a rhythmic reminder of the bleak weather outside.

Bruce sighed. "Honestly, I've been fed up with this weather. Two years post-divorce, living in a one-bedroom flat and I'm still trying to figure out what normal looks like. This grey, miserable start to the day? It feels like the world's just dragging me down."

John nodded quietly, watching the road. "Yeah. Starts like this make you want to hibernate, but keep your chin up mate."

Bruce kept his eyes on the road, but his mind drifted for a moment, turned and drove into The Emerald Pines Golf Club car park, just outside York. Waiting there was Eric and Steve, looking like drowned rats already. It was the kind of morning that made even the most dedicated golfers question their sanity. Rain hammered the greens, puddles spread like small lakes across the fairways, and the wind had an icy edge that sliced through jackets and pride alike.

"Morning lads, lovely weather". Bruce shouted across the near empty carpark, and headed to the first tee.

The soggy fairways stretched out before them as Bruce placed his tee into the ground. Turned and looked back towards the dimly lit clubhouse, shaking his head. The rain continued relentless, drumming against umbrellas and umbrellas that had already been ripped inside out by the gusts. The grass was soaked, the ground squelching with every step. Bruce stepped up confidently, despite the weather. His feet sank slightly into the mud as he gripped his driver. He took a deep breath, aimed, and swung. With a loud crack and a spray of mud, the ball soared—an impressive, mighty drive that cut through the rain-laden air and disappeared into the distance, almost defying how miserable the day was.

"Nice shot," John muttered, giving him a begrudging nod as Bruce grinned. "That's more like it, match that if you can!"

On the second hole, Steve was already in trouble. Clad in waterproofs, he was stomping around in a bunker, frustrated and cursing under his breath as he fought his way out of the mud. His club struck repeatedly at the sand; each shot more of a splash than anything precise.

"Are you serious?" Eric called, watching from a safe distance. "You treat that bunker like you're digging to Australia, get a grip man!"

Steve flung his arms up, a soggy glove flopping from his hand. "I swear, I've never seen a sand trap so stubborn. It's like the mud's got a hold of my club or something. I' don't know why I bother"

"Neither do we!" Laughed Eric. "Neither do we my lovely lad" as he walked towards the green.

Meanwhile, Bruce and John made decent progress on the third and fourth holes, their shots occasionally slipping and skidding on the wet turf but mostly staying playable—if not pretty. The balls hung low in the drizzle, their shiny surfaces dulled by mud and rain. The players' outfits were soaked through; their spirits dipped just a little lower with each hole.

By the sixth hole, the group was soaked through and more resigned than competitive. Bruce was still swinging with purpose, and he cracked a smile after a good shot—his ball landing on the fringe of the green with a satisfying splash of mud.

"Not bad, Bruce," John said, dragging his towel across his face—more mud than sweat. "If we weren't so soaked, I might even say you're having a good day."

Steve, emerging from another bunker with a mud-covered face, shot a wry grin. "Don't get too cocky. Just wait till the last hole, and I'll make sure I sink a triple just to remind you how miserable this morning truly is." They battled on through the course, holes blurring into one another—the relentless rain making green into mud, bunkers into potential swimming pools. Their laughter was muffled, mostly drowned out by the drizzle and wind.

Finally, on the 18th hole, the storm was at its worst. The wind howled around them, the rain driven sideways in icy sheets. Bruce swung hard, catching his shot just right, and the ball shot across the sky, finally curling toward the faint outline of the green. The others followed, all battered and soaked, each swing more about preserving what little pride they had left than any hope of a good score. As they trudged up the final fairway, their clubs weighed down with mud, Bruce looked toward the clubhouse—a distant silhouette against the grey sky. The thought of getting out of the rain and into the warmth was almost intoxicating.

They finally reached the edge of the green, dripping and exhausted, each of them muttering about the weather, their game, and how they'd probably be lucky if they scored double digits. Bruce looked down at his card, drops from his baseball cap dripping and smudging his scorecard. "Not too bad considering", he said out loud. Bruce, Steve, Eric, and John trudged back toward the clubhouse, clubs slung over shoulders, soaked to the bone and laughing like idiots.

"I think my socks are swimming," Steve muttered, pulling off his glove with a squelch. "I've got trout in my shoes."

Eric grunted. "If we were smart, we'd have stayed in bed."
John shook his head. "But then who'd listen to your cheerful commentary, Eric?"

Inside the clubhouse, the atmosphere was no different. The fire crackled quietly, casting warm, flickering shadows across the dim walls. The smell of damp wool and old wood mingled with the faint scent of stale coffee. The group dropped their clubs haphazardly near the door, inside the changing room they peeled off their waterproofs and shaking out the worst of the mud. Put on dry socks and shoes ready for action. Bruce bumped the door open and stepped inside the club lounge, the warmth a sharp contrast to the icy wind outside. He looked around at his friends, all damp, defeated but still grinning weakly.

"Not exactly a day for golf, my waterproofs weren't a lot of good out there today" Steve muttered, grinning despite himself as he rubbed his sodden sleeves.

Bruce looked around, a little surprised he didn't feel more defeated. Despite the miserable weather, there was a strange sense of camaraderie—something about sharing the same soggy battle that made every shot, every curse, every splash worth it. He stood there for a moment, dripping on the carpet, looking out through fogged windows at the miserable grey beyond. He paused, then he said it.

"I'm sick of this shitty weather. You know, once we're dried off—with a good drink—I'm going to bring up that trip to Thailand again. Sunlight, green fairways, no damn rain. We've earned it."

The others looked at him, acknowledgment flickering in their eyes

"I mean it, I'm sick of this shit" Bruce continued, voice sharp with a kind of clarity they hadn't heard in a while. "Week after week, we come out here, we freeze our arses off, and for what? To pretend we're having fun?"

Steve raised an eyebrow. "Careful, mate. You're the one who makes us come out here."

"I know," Bruce said, cracking a grin. "And I love it, really. Sorry to say that it's more that I'm with you lot, than the golf. But hear me out."

He leaned in. They knew that look — the same one he wore when he booked their annual Ryder Cup weekend or dragged them to that unforgettable trip to St Andrews.

"What we need," he said slowly, letting it land, "is a proper boys' trip. Thailand. Sunshine. Golf. Beers. Massage. The bloody works." There was a moment of silence. Then Eric blinked. "Thailand?"

John let out a low whistle. "From cold fairways to coconut cocktails. Sandra will be happy, she'll love that"

Bruce interjected. "No wives, this is a proper boy's trip. I've been looking into it. World-class courses. Tropical weather. A proper break."

Steve leaned back, worry creeping across his face. "I'm not sure mum would agree to this"

"For god's sake Steve, you're 45 years old, it's time you made decisions for yourself and stopped hiding behind your mum's apron! Plus, you never know, you might lose that cherry and finally get laid" Bruce said smirking.

The whole group burst into laughter as Steve turned a bright shade of red.

"I'll need to run this by Bev, she won't be happy." Eric announced. Bruce shot back, "Eric, you've been married twenty years — isn't it about time you grew a pair, and asked for permission to wear the pants?"

"I'll swing it, don't worry – I want to be on this trip, god we all need this trip" Eric replied.

"Sure mate, we all know Bev's the one who actually runs the show. Just let us know when she's given you Board approval and had it also signed off by the dog," Said John.

"Don't you worry boys, I'm bloody in for sure – she's not stopping this one!"

Bruce clapped his hands together. "Then it's settled. Let's swap wet greens for palm trees. What do you say, lads—one unforgettable trip?"

They raised their beers like a toast. The clubhouse buzzed around them, the sound of clinking cutlery and distant laughter. But at that table, something had shifted. The rain outside no longer mattered.

As the group settled into the warmth of the clubhouse, rubbing their arms and laughing at the miserable weather, another four-ball approached their table with a cheerful stride.

"You lot haven't been out in all that, have you?" Bernard asked, sipping his beer, a broad grin on his face. "While you crazy guys were out there in the rain, we've been down in the pro shop, using the simulator."

Bruce looked up, grinning. "Yeah, we were out there. Some of us are still men, a bit of rain doesn't worry us" he joked, rubbing the back of his neck. "You and your boys may have been dry, but I bet still slicing your shots."

Bernard chuckled. "That's right, mate. The real men—treating the weather like a challenge. We've been perfecting our swings on that fancy screen while you lot looked like drowned rats."

Danny shook his head, a smirk on his face. "No point risking more mud and misery when you've got a high-tech option sitting right there."

"Thailand is a lot better than that simulator" Bruce said with a wink.

"Trust me, you should give it a shot sometime. It's almost as good as the real thing—minus the soaking." Replied Bernard.

Bruce leaned forward, raising an eyebrow, a playful grin. "Speaking of trips- we are going to Thailand next month, so, are you lot interested in expanding it? Turning into a proper holiday?"

Keith, always up for a laugh, grinned and elbowed Rory. "Why not? Me, Rory, and Dan—our little gang—will come along.

Make it a proper week instead of just golf. We were thinking Portugal, but this sounds better, and It'd be a laugh."

Everyone looked at Bernard and the others, sharing amused glances. "Don't you need permission from that young Russian filly of yours," Steve said, smirking. "I do what we want around here, she has no say in it – so I'm in, and she's Ukrainian, not Russian!"

Bruce shot him a sideways smirk. "Excellent. Looking like a real trip now!"

Laughter bubbled up again as the banter continued. Despite the miserable weather outside, the camaraderie inside kept their spirits buoyed—reminding them what drew them here, rain or shine.

Bruce looked around at the damp but cheerful faces. "It's good to have plans," he said softly. "Something to look forward to, who wants another pint?"

With that, Craig the Club Pro swaggered in. He was a man who really fancied himself, stuck in the 80s and a dress sense of Sonny Crockett from Miami Vice. He was a reasonable golf coach, but couldn't make it on tour as he had the yips.

"What's going on fellas?" He asked as he sipped his blended fruit smoothie.

"We're all going on a golfing trip to Thailand, Greens. Beers. Massage - and who knows what" Replied Bruce laughing.

"Please Bruce, don't say that to Mum," said Steve.

"Sounds like fun, room for one more" asked Craig.

"Sure, more the merrier," Bruce said with a grin. "In fact, I'm also planning to ask Stu—he's in Hong Kong—and Josh, over in Dubai. Josh is loaded, so money won't be a problem. Stu — he'll give you a good run for your money, Craig. He was on the second tour back in his twenties, really great player."

He took a step forward, waving his arm in the air as he headed towards the bar. "And boys, all the caddies in Thailand are females!" he added, and they all cheered, their voices loud and full of teasing excitement.

Chapter Two

The Fairway to Patong

Bruce sat at his computer, coffee in hand, eyes narrowed like a man choosing a new putter. The screen glowed with a dozen tabs open: hotels, flights, golf courses, travel insurance, this was given the precision of a military operation. He had a highlighter in one hand and a printer grinding in the background like it was fighting for its life. He sipped his coffee and spoke aloud to himself.

"Right... if this lot are going to Thailand, it's going to need a bit of strategy. And by strategy, I mean three hotel options and a map of where the action is."

Five pages slid out of the printer, slightly crooked. He tapped them into a neat stack, admired his work, then said the only thing a man says before kicking off a midlife golf tour halfway around the world: "Let chaos begin." At the clubhouse, the rain was falling sideways again and the windows steamed with the smell of bacon butties and stale beer. Steve, Eric, and John were huddled at their usual table.

"Here he is," Steve said as Bruce arrived, documents in hand like an over-excited travel agent who specialised in bad ideas. Bruce dropped the printouts on the table with a thud.

"Gentlemen. Welcome to your future."

Eric raised an eyebrow. "Looks like homework."

Bruce ignored him. "We're going to Thailand — Patong Beach to be exact — and I've got three hotels. Each one more dangerous than the last."

"Dangerous?" said John, squinting at the pages. "Do they not have lifts?"

Bruce grinned. "No, I mean the kind of danger that involves cheap cocktails, inappropriate karaoke, and regrettable WhatsApp photos, and the possibility you'll need a shot of penicillin."

Eric looked nervous already. "Bev's got alerts on my phone."

"Then use Keith's," John said. "He's off the grid."

"I have email," John muttered. Bruce cleared his throat dramatically and began.

"Option One: The Royal Orchid Resort. Right on the beach, two pools, and a breakfast buffet that runs until midday."
"Ooh," John said. "That's civilised."

"Option Two: Patong Heights. Adults only. Rooftop bar. Infinity pool. Probably comes with a therapist."
Eric whistled. "That's more like it."

"Option Three: The Wild Lotus. Right off Bangla Road. No kids. No rules. Probably no towels either. It even offers — and I quote — 'the option for joiners to enter your room' on their website."

Steve squinted. "Joiners? What the hell do we need a bloody joiner for? We're not building a patio."

The table burst into laughter. Eric, quick to join in, shouted, "What about electricians then? Seems unfair!" Even John chuckled, though he wasn't quite sure what a joiner did or what it meant in this context.

Bruce, barely able to speak through his grin, wiped a tear from his eye. "Different kind of joiner, lads. Different kind of... joining."

"Ohhh," John said slowly, then raised both eyebrows. "Right. Joiners. Gotcha."

Steve looked confused again. "Like a singles' night?"

"Something like that," Bruce smirked. "Let's just say it's very... guest friendly."

"What's Bangla Road?" asked Steve

Bruce lit up like a teenager discovering tequila. "Bangla Road, my friend, is the Vegas Strip of Thailand. A neon-soaked road of bars, music, madness, and enough questionable life choices to fill a trilogy."

Rory frowned. "Is it near a temple?"

Bruce paused. "In a sense... but the only worship happening there is at the altar of Chang and exotic dancers."

John was already sold. "Wild Lotus. All day. Let's ruin our reputations."

Steve looked panicked. "Does it have Wi-Fi? I'll need to be able to VC Mum."

"Mate," Bruce said, "you won't be caring about VC when you're down Bangla."

Bernard held up a hand. "Is your mum going to ask if it's cultural, Steve." Laughing.

Bruce didn't miss a beat. "It is. Thai culture. Street food. Night markets. Buddhist shrines. Ladyboys in feathered headdresses. It's very... layered."

Eric sighed. "We'll need a code word in case Bev calls. Something that sounds respectable, if Bev calls."

"Easy," Bruce said. "We say we're staying at a wellness retreat near a waterfall, no wifi. That covers everything. Including the hangovers." They all laughed — even Steve, though quietly and with some concern.

"Alright," Bruce said, spreading out the maps like a war general. "Vote time. Royal Orchid for comfort, Patong Heights for vibe, Wild Lotus for full throttle."

There was a moment of silence. Then, one by one, hands went up for Wild Lotus.

Bruce grinned. "Boys… we're going in, wrap up well."

There was a massive cheer around the group, except for Steve who looked like he was about to have root canal!
Bruce rubbed his hands together like a man about to steal Christmas.

"Right then, passports. I need your details today — don't make me chase you. I'll get everything booked this week. Flights, hotel, tee times, and maybe a few… joiners."
They all snorted.

"And," Bruce added, "once it's booked, I'll let you know what the damage is. You lot can cough up the cash. I'm not the Bank of bloody Thailand."

Steve nodded. "Fine by me. As long as I'm not sharing a room with Eric and his 11pm hot milk."

Eric folded his arms. "That's to settle my stomach, actually." Bruce waved them down. "No, we all have our own rooms. Oh, and one more thing — we've got a quick stopover in Dubai to collect Josh."

"Dubai?" John blinked. "Isn't that in the wrong direction?"

Bruce rolled his eyes. "Don't be soft, lad. I know your world map ends at Benidorm but trust me — it's en-route."

Steve leaned forward. "Wait... Josh? Josh-from-Uni Josh?"

Bruce grinned. "The very same. Lives out there now. Drives a ridiculous car, owns more loafers than sense, and probably hasn't carried his own golf clubs since 2012. Works in finance. You know, the sort who wears sunglasses indoors and says things like 'synergy' without shame."

Eric winced. "I bet he'll be in the pointy end."

Bruce nodded solemnly. "Business class, of course. Probably sipping champagne while we're wrestling with a tray of lasagna and someone's knees in our backs. But don't worry — he's buying the beers when we land."

"Fair trade," Steve said.

Bruce pulled out another sheet from his folder. "Now. The real magic. The golf."

He laid out a week-long schedule like it was sacred scripture.

"Day one: Red Canyon Golf Club — carved into the hills, stunning views, very forgiving for those of us who play like pirates.

"Day two: Pheonix Dunes"

"Isn't that the one has a 18th hole shaped like a dragon's head. No one knows why." Steve asked.

"Bloody name Pheonix might have something to do with it, you soft lad," Said Craig.

"Good point!" Replied Steve, looking sheepish.

"Then we've got a free day, thought you'd all need to recover" John's eyes lit up. "I'm sure you'll come up with something bordering on illegal for us to do that day, Brewster". Bruce winked at him, and then carried on with the list.

"Then Lakeside Pines, Tiger Falls course, and to cap it off — the legendary Blue Mountain, championship level, water hazards everywhere. Bring spare balls and a sense of humour.

The lads stared at the itinerary like it was the holy grail.
Bruce sat back, arms behind his head, grinning from ear to ear. "Lads, this is going to be one hell of a trip. The kind of week we'll still be talking about in years to come. Possibly at our retirement homes. Possibly during physiotherapy. Either way — unforgettable."

They all nodded slowly. Then, as if by some sacred Saturday tradition, Steve raised his half-drunk pint of larger.

"To Thailand."
"To Thailand," they echoed.

The rain outside no longer mattered. Bruce was back home that evening, sat in front of his laptop in joggers and a T-shirt that had definitely seen better decades. He poked at a chicken chow mien from the local takeaway with one hand while, frantically hammering flight details into the keyboard with the other. His living room looked like a travel agency had exploded — printouts, golf brochures, and a suspiciously sticky Post-it with the words "Check if Wild Lotus has irons (golf or otherwise?)" scrawled across it.

He picked up his phone and called Josh. "Alright, globe-trotter," Bruce said as soon as Josh answered. "You need to be on flight Middle Star MS375 out of Dubai. Land in Phuket — try not to look too smug when you walk past us from business class."

Josh chuckled. "I'll try to keep the champagne glass low, mate. Can't wait — been dying for a proper lads' trip. I'll sort my own hotel; I can't slum it with you lot"

Bruce updated the spreadsheet with military precision, then moved onto the final call of the night: Stu in Hong Kong. Stu answered halfway through a beer, as always. "What's happening, chief?" "All systems go," Bruce said. "Flights booked, hotel sorted, tee times confirmed. We'll stop in Dubai to grab Josh. Landing in Phuket on the Sunday."

"Brilliant," Stu said. "Craig's coming, right?" "Yep, he's in. Already practicing his backswing and pretending he's not going to get hammered on day one."

"Thank God," Stu sighed. "Maybe I'll finally get a decent round in, instead of playing with you hackers who think 'birdie' means 'some chick dancing on a bar'. I'm bringing my A-game this time."

Bruce snorted. "You've been threatening your A-game for ten years."

"Yeah, and one day it'll show up. Just like your six-pack." Stu replied

Bruce grinned, stretched, and leaned back in his chair. Flights, hotel, golf — done. Group chats would go mental tomorrow, and no doubt Eric would have questions about the minibar policy. But tonight? It was sorted; this was happening.
And it was going to be legendary.

Bruce woke the next morning feeling like a man on a mission. Just one final box to tick. He glanced at the clock — nearly 8 a.m. in Yorkshire, which meant it was beer o'clock in Thailand. Perfect.

He hit call on Pete – Golf Nut. It rang twice before Pete answered, the unmistakable hum of a busy bar spilling through the phone. Laughter, clinking glasses... and definitely some high-pitched giggling in the background.

"Brucey!" Pete shouted over the noise. "Hang on, I'll pop outside— actually, screw that. It's happy hour. Don't want to lose my seat."

Bruce laughed. "Living the dream, mate. Just checking we're good for Blue Mountain."

"All sorted," Pete replied. "Got the member rate lined up. Bit of a discount — more cash for beers."

"And girls, by the sound of it," Bruce said, grinning. "What's that racket behind you?"

Pete chuckled. "Just lining up a few for the boys. Thought I'd get ahead of the game and interview a few before you lot arrive."

"They won't know what's hit them," Bruce said.

"Speaking of which," Pete added casually, "did I mention… it's Songkran that week?"

Bruce blinked. "The water festival?"

"Yep. Whole country turns into a giant water fight. It'll be wet in more ways than one."

Bruce smirked. "Bloody hell. Forgot that." Then he paused. "You know what? I won't tell the lads. Wouldn't want to spoil the surprise."

"Evil," Pete said, laughing.

"Strategic," Bruce replied. "See you soon, mate."

He hung up, sat back, and grinned. Golf, sun, beer, women —
and now a national water fight. This trip was shaping up to be
epic.

Chapter Three

Cold Hands, Warm Lies

A few weeks out from take-off, and the rain had finally given Yorkshire a break — but the cold hadn't. It was the March Medal, held on Saturday at Emerald Pines Golf Club, and the lads were out in force, wrapped up like arctic explorers.

"Remind me again why we do this to ourselves," muttered Steve, blowing warm air into his hands, standing over his ball on the 3rd tee. He was wearing two pairs of socks, a snood and woolly hat that looked like his mother had knitted it.

"Are you wearing thermal leggings?" asked Eric.

"No, I've put a pair of my Mum tights on to keep warm" Steve chirped back.

"That's bloody tragic mate, trying to tell us something?" Eric quipped back.

"We do it because we're a bunch a sado's." chimed in Bruce. "Fear ye not though boys, Patong has sunshine and cold beer waiting. Anyway, the important thing today lads is to keep an eye on that cheating twat Sanderson. He won last time, but we know he cheated"

"Cool your engines Bruce, it's only a game," said Steve

Eric pulled a tee out of his bag with numb fingers. "Yep, just think lads — in a few weeks we'll be sweating in shorts and sipping Chang with a view of palm trees."

John, dressed as if he were heading to Everest base camp, said nothing. His tee shot had just bounced off a tree, into a bunker, then somehow out again and onto the path.

"Shot of the day," Bruce said dryly.

They slogged through the front nine with frozen fingers and sarcastic encouragement. By the 12th hole, someone's whiskey flask made an appearance, and by the 15th, laughter had replaced complaining. Patong was getting closer.

Back in the clubhouse, drinks in hand and cheeks glowing, Bruce pulled out his battered itinerary folder and laid it on the table. "Everything's locked in, lads. Flights, hotels, golf — the works." The table murmured with approval, until Eric shifted awkwardly in his seat.

Bruce narrowed his eyes. "Eric?"

Eric coughed. "All good. Looks brilliant."

"You told Bev yet?" Steve asked.

Eric hesitated. "Not… exactly."

John burst out laughing. "Mate! It's been weeks! What are you waiting for, a written invitation from the dog?"

"Don't worry," Eric said, trying to sound confident. "I've got a plan."

Bruce raised an eyebrow. "That's what you said last year when you tried to hide your new putter behind the washing machine."

"Yeah," John added, "and she found it before the first spin cycle."

"She won't mind," Eric said, waving them off. "I'll just ease her into it. Nice dinner, glass of wine, maybe let her watch Call the Midwife. Then—bam! —mention it casually."

"She'll kill you," Bruce said, grinning.

"She'll be too busy going out with her mates and leaving me with that bloody dog" Eric muttered.

"Well," Steve said, raising his pint, "here's to Bev's social life — the only reason Eric still plays golf."

They all laughed and clinked glasses. Thailand was just around the corner. And Eric? He had about two weeks to gain permission and ensure the survival of his marriage.

At that precise moment, the clubhouse door creaked open, and in walked Bernard — sixty-four, twice divorced, and currently punching several leagues above his weight with his twenty-something girlfriend, Sasha, clinging to his arm like she'd just won a sugar daddy raffle. Bruce clocked them immediately. He leaned in, grinning.

"Wonder if he's told her yet he's coming with us."

"No chance," said Steve. "She'll have him doing spa days and Instagram selfies. My bet's firmly on he hasn't mentioned it at all."

"Or," John chimed in, "he's booked her ticket and told her we're all going to a couples' retreat in the Himalayas."

Bernard spotted them, gave a small wave, and after parking Sasha at their table with an espresso martini and her third selfie of the afternoon, sauntered over. He carried that usual Bernard swagger — somewhere between used car dealer and game show host — and his cologne hit them before he did.

"All right, lads?" he said, adjusting his collar. "Everything sorted?"

Bruce raised an eyebrow. "Told her yet, then?"

Bernard didn't flinch. "I have. She threw a little wobbler."

"And?" John asked, eyes wide.

Bernard shrugged. "I simply told her, 'If you don't like it, you can piss off back to the Supermarket checkout job in Kiev.'"

The table howled.

John blinked. "Wait — she was working in a supermarket when you met?"

"Indeed," Bernard said proudly. "Online, of course. Checkout girl in Kiev. I ordered a box of almonds — got myself a red-hot chick instead."

Bruce nearly choked on his pint. "You met Sasha on a website while she was scanning cabbages in Ukraine?"

"Global logistics, Bruce," Bernard replied. "Some lads order golf balls. I import girlfriends."

Steve wheezed. "What delivery option did you choose — next day air or cargo hold. Can you also give me that website?"

Bernard smirked, clearly chuffed with himself. "It's called Chernobyl of Love, Steve. But lads, it's all about knowing your worth."

"With wisdom like that," Eric muttered, "it's a miracle you're not buried in a shallow grave somewhere."

Bernard gave a theatrical wink and sauntered back to Sasha, who was now on her phone, probably Googling "luxury handbags UK."

John leaned back. "This trip's going to be chaos."

Bruce grinned. "And we haven't even made it to the airport yet."

Taking a long sip of his pint, looked around the table with that familiar glint in his eye, and clapped his hands together.

"Right then, lads — I'm heading to the York Designer Outlet this afternoon. Going to get myself fully kitted out for Thailand. New polos, some of those fancy lightweight golf trousers, and maybe a pair of Ray-Bans if the price is right. Anyone coming?"

Steve didn't even look up from his sausage sandwich. "No need, mate. My Mum's already sorted me."

Bruce raised an eyebrow. "Your mum, did she use Gratton's Catalogue?"

"Nah, she sorted me with a trip to town," Steve said, completely unbothered. "Once I told her we were going on the trip, and she'd stopped fainting, she went into full prep mode. Came back from Boots like she was outfitting me for jungle warfare. Got a multipack of mosquito repellent sprays, after-bite sticks, anti-itch cream, and some tablets that apparently stop your blood tasting nice to insects. She's also got me factor 50 suncream"

Eric leaned in. "Your blood tastes nice to insects?"

"Apparently so," Steve said, shrugging. "Mum reckons it's because I eat too much sugar. She even got me a sun hat with one of those little neck flaps. Looks like I'm leading a desert expedition."

Bruce laughed. "You'll be the only one in Patong who looks like he's lost on a school geography trip."

"Mum's even laminated my travel insurance details and booked me in for a pre-flight pedicure," Steve added.
Bruce nearly spat out his beer. "A what?"

"She says she's not having me showing up in Thailand with 'feet like a builder's elbow." The table roared with laughter.

"Unbelievable," Bruce said, wiping his eyes. "And I thought I was overprepared." He looked at John and said, "Any chance he's actually batting for the other team?"

"Each to their own" replied John.

"I'm telling you," Steve said, completely deadpan, "you haven't lived until you've had your cuticles massaged while listening to Enya in a reclining chair."

Bruce chuckled. "So, your mum's sorted your wardrobe, your nails and medicine cabinet, lucky lad!"

"Sandra also sorted me, and told me she would do the packing too, she's such a sweetheart" John said chuckling. "I'm going with three pairs of cargo shorts, six moisture-wicking golf polos in 'tropical tones' — her words, not mine.

Bruce stood up, laughing. "Well, I'll go and do it the old-fashioned way — panic buy stuff I don't need, forget underwear, and spend too much on a belt I'll never wear again."

Eric looked thoughtful. "Can you grab me a pair of golf socks while you're there? Size nine. But only if they're breathable — Bev always says my feet smell like damp compost."

Bruce groaned. "Why do I feel like I'm taking a group of Year 6 kids on a school trip?"

"Because you are," Steve grinned, and with that, Bruce drained the rest of his pint and set off on his solo mission. By the time he pulled into the outlet mall car park, the clouds had parted, and the Yorkshire sun was doing its best to pretend it was spring. Bruce marched through the automatic doors like a man on a purpose-driven pilgrimage — only his holy grail involved linen shirts, breathable pants, and anything labelled UV-protective. Inside, he made a beeline for the golf store, where an attractive assistant in tight chinos and a name badge that read Chloe greeted him with a smile.

"Holiday shopping?" she asked, watching him eye up a rack of moisture-wicking polo shirts in colours no sane man would usually wear.

"Thailand," Bruce said, puffing out his chest a little. "Golf trip. Bit of business. Mostly mischief."

Chloe grinned. "Well, you've come to the right place."

Twenty minutes later, Bruce had somehow agreed that he needed three polos ("You'll want variety in the humidity"), two pairs of shorts ("These ones breathe!"), a pack of golf gloves ("The grip in that heat is crucial"), and a cap with a built-in sweatband ("Stylish and sensible"). Before he knew it, Chloe had him trying on a pair of wraparound sunglasses and convincing him that he looked "very PGA Tour with a hint of Bond villain." Bruce, naturally, bought two pairs. From there, things escalated quickly. A stop in the sportswear shop for "just a look" turned into new trainers, bamboo socks, and a fancy gym towel he'd never use. In the outdoors shop, he somehow walked out with a packable rain poncho ("Just in case Songkran gets too wet") and a head torch he couldn't explain.

By the time he'd hit the cologne shop, grabbed a duty-free-sized bottle of aftershave "for the ladies," and picked up some novelty boxer shorts with cartoon tuk-tuks on them, he looked like he was preparing for an expedition up Everest — not a lads' trip to Patong Beach. He finally emerged through the glass doors of the outlet two hours later, arms heavy and triumphant, dragging six oversized shopping bags behind him like a man returning from battle. A passing teenager gave him a sideways look. Bruce just grinned.

"Preparation," he said out loud, to absolutely no one. "That's the difference between a good holiday… and a legendary one." He tossed the bags into the boot of his car, slammed it shut with a grin, and pulled out his phone.

"Boys," he said into the group chat voice message. "Mission accomplished. I am officially kitted up, dangerous, and ready for tropical mayhem. Patong better be ready, especially those ladies!"

Upstairs in his room, Steve was neatly folding his freshly purchased holiday gear. On the bed lay a full spread of bold, tropical prints — shirts covered in flamingos, pineapples, and one pair of particularly offensive lime green Hawaiian shorts emblazoned with hibiscus flowers and tiny surfboards.

He held the shorts up, admired them with a quiet, satisfied nod, then folded them like sacred linen. "Patong won't know what's hit it," he muttered to himself, placing them delicately beside his bottle of mosquito repellent and a full-size tube of factor 50 sun cream — both purchased by his mum, of course.

Downstairs, Gloria was in full cleaning mode. A no-nonsense Yorkshire woman in her late sixties, she had the sharpness of a court barrister and the emotional range of a 90s sitcom matriarch. Since her divorce fifteen years ago, she'd run her household with military precision — and Steve, at 45, was still the loyal corporal under her command.

As she wiped down the kitchen counter with industrial strength lemon cleaner, Steve's phone buzzed loudly beside the fruit bowl. Gloria glanced over. Her eyes narrowed. One message. Then another. Then a third — a voice note. Curious (and a little suspicious of anything titled "Fore Play"), she tapped it, Steve had never been able to figure out how to password protect his phone!

"Boys. Mission accomplished. I am officially kitted up, dangerous, and ready for tropical mayhem. Patong better be ready — especially those ladies."

Gloria stopped wiping. She blinked slowly. Like a python sizing up its prey. Her lips pursed with the force of ten thousand unspoken judgments.

"Dangerous?" she muttered. "Oh, he's about as dangerous as a sausage roll." The door creaked. Steve came padding downstairs in socks and a faded Gleneagles t-shirt, carrying his prized Hawaiian shorts.

"Mum, have you seen—"

"Sit down," Gloria said, holding his phone like it had just confessed to a felony. "We need a word."

"What's up?"

She pressed play again.
"…Patong better be ready — especially those ladies."

Steve went pale. "Oh no…"
"Oh yes," Gloria snapped. "What exactly do you and your little band of middle-aged misfits think you're doing? I bought you that factor 50 so you don't come back looking like a boiled

beetroot — not so you can parade around Thailand like a second-rate Tom Jones."

"Mum, it's just a joke—"

"Fore Play? Honestly, Steven. You're going on a golfing holiday, not starring in a midlife crisis documentary."

Steve tried to protest, but she was already mid-rant.

"I'll tell you this: if I see one photo of you with a cocktail in each hand, wearing those vulgar shorts, and dancing with some poor innocent Thai lady who thinks you're a minor celebrity from 'Emmerdale' — I will march down to that travel agency and fly out there myself."

She handed the phone back with a flourish. "And don't think I don't know what 'joiners welcome' means. I wasn't born yesterday."

Steve clutched his shorts like a man defending his last shred of dignity. "I'm 45, Mum."

"And you'll be 46 and grounded if I see glitter on your chest."

Upstairs again, safely back in the sanctuary of his room, Steve slumped on the bed, defeated. His Hawaiian shorts lay limp across his knees like crushed dreams. He picked up his phone, sighed, and opened the group chat: Fore Play.

He typed slowly, like a man issuing a formal apology.

Steve: Lads… minor situation. Mum might have heard the Patong message. She's not… thrilled. Might need to tone things down. Temporarily.

A reply pinged back instantly.

Bruce: What happened? Did she cancel your pocket money – actually we know, she sent us a message. Check this chat line?

Craig: Tell her to come with us — she'd be wild on Bangla Road after three Mai Tais.

John: Please don't bring your mum, Steve. I'm fragile enough already.

Eric: If Steve's grounded, does that mean I'm no longer the most pathetic one in the group?

Bruce: Not so fast Eric — your dog-sitting curfew still wins.

Steve groaned and typed again.

Steve: She threatened to fly out if I "start behaving like Tom Jones." And yes, she's seen the "joiners welcome" comment. She's terrifying. The chat exploded:

Craig: Please tell me she doesn't know what joiners are.

Steve: She absolutely does. She said, "I wasn't born yesterday," then told me I'd be grounded if she sees glitter on my chest or in my boxer shorts.

Bruce: I don't know what's funnier — the glitter or the fact she thinks you could pull a joiner.

John: At least you've got someone checking in on you. My mum's too busy re-watching Midsomer Murders.

Bernard: My brother just read over my shoulder and said if there are joiners, there better be plumbers too. I'm not even sure what that means – is he gay all of a sudden?

Bruce: Lads, I'm crying. Also, new rule: Anyone caught texting their mum before, during or after this trip buys the first round at every bar.

Craig: Deal.

Steve: Fine. But I'm wearing the shorts. She can't ban my shorts.

Bruce: Do what you want, mate. Just don't blame us when the locals run screaming from the lime green nightmare.

Steve smiled faintly. The shorts were back on the bed. Loud. Proud. Unapologetically offensive. He picked them up, folded them one more time.

Bruce: Bus leaves 3am sharp tomorrow, outside Sparks supermarket on the Highstreet - No messing about.

Craig: Not waiting if Anyone's late. You're on your own if you miss it.

Steve: Especially you, Eric. Told Bev yet?

Eric: ...I'm working on it.

John: Mate, we fly early morning. What are you waiting for —
divine intervention?

Bruce: Hope you like explaining your suitcase in the garage.

Eric: Don't worry. I'll be there.

Steve: That's not what we asked.

Eric: I won't be late. See you there, fellas.

Craig: Not if Bev sees your boarding pass first 😄

Bruce: Just bring the dog with you. Say it's a pet therapy
retreat.

Eric: She won't even notice I'm gone till she's recovered from
her hangover tomorrow.

John: Famous last words, mate...

Bruce: This time Sunday, lads. Patong will never be the same again.

Steve: Patong be ready. Especially those ladies 😌

He then ran out of his bedroom and into the bathroom.

Gloria: (Steve's Mum): This is Gloria. You're all a bunch of perverts leading my poor innocent Steven astray!

Bruce: 😄

Craig: Oh. My. God.

Eric: Steve, your mum just called us perverts.

John: That's because we are perverts.

Steve: I just popped to the loo, left my phone on the bed and she's sneaked in. She's relentless 😳

Bruce: Rookie move. Gloria's got admin rights now.

Craig: 😂 😂 😂 Steve's mum thinks we are all perverts, cracks me up.

Bruce: Trip of a lifetime, and we've already been grounded by Steve's mother. 😂 😂

Chapter Four

Wheels Up, Warnings Down

The alarm buzzed like a crazed mosquito on steroids, but Bruce was already half-awake, grinning in the darkness like a kid on Christmas morning. His eyes snapped open. No confusion. No groaning. Just one word pounding in his head like a bass drum:

Thailand.

He sprang out of bed like a man twenty years younger, feet hitting the floor with purpose, arms stretched high like he'd just scored at Wembley.

"Let's have it, you saucy mare!" he shouted into the room, fist-pumping the air like he'd just won the lottery. Yorkshire might be wet, cold and miserable, but Bruce? Bruce was flying to bloody Thailand. Adrenaline now doing the job of a double espresso, he stumbled toward the shower, mumbling about sun, golf, and how many beers you could technically drink before lunch.

Over at Steve's house, things were already in full swing. Gloria was up, dressed, and working the frying pan like it was a military mission. A full English sizzled on the plate: eggs, bacon, sausage, beans, toast, black pudding, and a grilled tomato no one ever asked for.

"You can't be going all that way without a good breakfast," she insisted, slapping the plate in front of Steve with motherly authority. "And don't eat any of that foreign muck, you hear me? I've packed the diarrhea tablets in your wash bag. You know what your stomach's like — can't even handle Skegness."

Steve, already dressed in his oversized Hawaiian shorts and a fresh white polo, gave her a sheepish nod. "Yes, Mum."

She handed him a Ziploc bag packed with various remedies — pills for travel sickness, indigestion, heat rash, dehydration, and something called 'emergency electrolytes. "I'm not having you ruin your bowels in a country where I can't shout at someone about it," she warned. "And before you go, get into proper trousers, it's cold out there and you can save your shorts for the holiday.

"Yes mum, he said" walking upstairs and changing into jeans and a shirt.

Once changed, he pecked and hugged his mother, and walked to the door and headed for the bus.

Meanwhile, over at John's house, the morning was calm and still, save for the faint gurgle of the kettle in the kitchen. John descended the stairs in his usual cautious fashion, clutching the banister like it might vanish. He placed his neatly packed suitcase by the front door beside his golf clubs, both items standing like obedient dogs ready for a walk.

His wife, Sandra, was at the counter making coffee, still in her dressing gown. Without turning, she said, "Sit down, love. Got something for you."

John yawned, scratched his neck, and slumped into the chair. She placed a steaming mug in front of him—and then, quite deliberately, set a small packet on the table beside it.

John squinted at the packet. "What are these for?"

Sandra folded her arms. "Look, love. You haven't had a proper holiday with the lads in years. And I know what goes on in these places—don't try and play innocent."

John blinked, his face reddening. "But I—"

She held up a hand. "I'm not saying go mad. I'm just saying, if something does happen, I don't want you bringing anything back. Or worse, some Thai lovely turning up at our door in ten months holding a baby and a copy of your passport."

John's jaw moved but no words came out. She leaned in, kissed him on the head, and added with a smirk, "Just be careful. And have fun."

He nodded slowly, wide-eyed. "Right... fun. Yes. Of course." Sandra picked up the mug, took a sip, I'll drop you off, you can't walk all that way, and a taxi now is hard to find at this hour.

She then walked out, leaving John alone at the table—staring down at the condoms like they were part of some pop quiz he hadn't revised for.

Over at Bernard's house, steam billowed out of the en-suite as he stepped from the shower, towel slung low, and hair slicked back like a man clinging to the last flickers of his prime. He paddled into the bedroom, humming to himself, only to freeze in his tracks.

Sasha was there. Wearing very little. And looking like trouble. Draped across the bed in full, sultry Ukrainian glamour, she locked eyes with him. Her voice, thick with accent and intention, rolled out like velvet.

"Baby… I want to make sure you don't have any sexy thoughts while you are away…" She leaned back, lips parted just slightly. "…so come and make love to me now." Bernard's jaw practically unhinged.

"Hold that thought, sweetheart!" he blurted, doing a swift pirouette on the carpet.

He darted to the nightstand drawer, flinging it open with the urgency of a man defusing a bomb.

"Where the hell are the blue tablets?" he muttered, grabbing a glass of water with one hand and rummaging with the other.

"You don't drop lines like that when I'm this close to boarding a plane."

Behind him, Sasha giggled softly. Bernard found the prized pill, downed it like a shot of tequila, and turned back around, puffing his chest.

"Right then… Operation Focused Departure has just been delayed." He marched toward the bed like a man on a mission, towel flapping behind him like a war flag.

Meanwhile, Bruce strolled up the street with a swagger in his step, golf clubs clattering behind him, suitcase rolling in tow, and a grin that said. "I'm early—and I know it."

The coach sat humming gently by the kerb, hazard lights blinking in the dull glow of the pre-dawn sky. He took a breath of the crisp morning air, stretching like a man about to conquer Everest. He dropped his bag and clubs on the pavement with a grunt. The coach driver, bleary-eyed but efficient, gave him a nod and promptly began lifting them into the undercarriage storage. Just as Bruce stepped toward the bus, one foot on the step, the low, guttural purr of an engine cut through the still morning air. A silver soft-top Mercedes whipped around the corner and pulled up at an angle right in front of the coach, tyres kissing the curb like a Hollywood arrival.

Out popped Bernard, grinning like a Cheshire cat, still buttoning his shirt and practically glowing with smug satisfaction. He walked to the back of the car, pulled his clubs and suitcase from the boot, and waved to the departing car.

From the driver's seat, Sasha leaned out in a silk robe, blowing a kiss.

"I love you, my darling!" she purred in her thick Ukrainian accent before speeding off into the dawn with the roof still down.

Bruce blinked. "Hardly bloody weather for the top down, Bernie."

Bernard winked as he sauntered up beside him. "Don't you worry, my son. She needs to cool off after the leaving present I just gave her."

Bruce barked a laugh, clapping him on the back. "You're an animal."

"She insisted, mate. Said she didn't want me having 'sexy thoughts' abroad... so she took care of it." He gave a theatrical sigh. "I'm practically limping." The two men chuckled.

Just as Bruce lifted his foot to the step again, a muffled tapping came from the window. Then again—faster. He looked up. Steve was there, forehead pressed to the glass like a Labrador in a thunderstorm, grinning like an idiot and waving furiously.

Bruce frowned. "What the hell...?" He stepped aboard, brushing past the automatic doors as they hissed behind him. As his eyes adjusted to the dim interior lighting, he looked down the aisle... and paused. Everyone was already there, except for Eric. Bernard gave a slow clap from behind him, nodding approvingly.

"So, where the hell is he?" asked Bruce, looking down the aisle and out through the tinted glass.

"I knew he'd bottle it," laughed Steve. "She's probably chained him to the bloody radiator or locked him in his bedroom."

The others chuckled, but Danny, who was perched near the back, squinted through the murky early dawn. "Hang on... someone's running." Everyone turned.

"He's here! He's bloody here!" Danny shouted, as a flailing figure in a hoodie and cargo shorts bolted across the supermarket car park, dragging a wheeled suitcase behind him like it was clinging for dear life, and clubs on his back. The bus door hissed open and in barrelled Eric, puffing like a steam train. His suitcase clattered onto the floor, and he chucked his golf bag in after it before diving into an empty seat and ducking like he was avoiding sniper fire. Bruce turned in his seat.

"What's up, mate?"

Eric wiped his brow, breathing heavily. "Right... let's get bloody moving. Sharpish. Before she wakes up."

John raised an eyebrow. "Wait, what?"

Eric glanced around, voice dropping to a whisper.

"I snuck out while she was still comatose from the prosecco she had last night with her mates. Left a note on the fridge."

Rory leaned forward. "A note?"

"Yeah. Said I'd gone to a spiritual retreat. Be back in a week or two." There was a pause. Bruce stared at him, eyes wide and chuckling.

"You're bloody joking. She'll literally kill you when she gets hold of you."

Eric gave a half-hearted shrug and a weak grin. "Nah, she'll have calmed down by the time I get back. Or moved on. Either way…"

Craig patted him on the back "You're a legend mate, a bloody legend.

Steve cackled. "What are you gonna do when she sees your tan and all those hotel receipts?"

Eric leaned his head back on the seat and sighed. "Cross that international incident when I come to it." The driver started the engine with a low rumble.

Bernard stretched out his legs, still smirking. "Right, lads. Phuket awaits. Literally and figuratively."

A cheer erupted from the group. As the coach pulled away into the dusky morning, nine middle-aged men—some single, some not, and one who might be by the time he got back—set off on the kind of trip that stories, legends, and questionable WhatsApp messages are made of.

Next stop: Manchester Airport, Terminal 1. Let the carnage begin. Bruce thought to himself as he sat back in his seat.

It didn't take long before the cans were cracking open—lager, cider, and a suspiciously cheap fizzy drink Steve insisted was "local craft." Laughter echoed through the bus as the lads toasted to freedom, friendship, and no wives or girlfriends for a solid week.

After a few hours, they rolled up to Manchester Airport. The usual chaos of holidaymakers mixed with last-minute shoppers swarming around. The boys checked in smoothly, albeit with Bruce almost forgetting his passport and Eric still nervously clutching his "spiritual retreat" excuse note. Through security, all went fairly smoothly—except for Steve.

"Oi, Steve, you alright?" Bruce called as Steve was pulled aside. A security officer gestured for Steve to follow him.

"We'll see you at the bar," Bruce shouted, grinning. "Message me, yeah?"

Steve gave a weak thumbs-up, a bit pale but trying to keep the banter alive. Minutes later, Steve found himself in a small, sterile room under harsh fluorescent lighting. The security man eyed him seriously.

"Sir, we've been given a tip-off. We need you to strip for a full security check."

Steve blinked. "Tip-off? About what?"

The officer didn't answer but motioned toward a privacy screen.

Back at the bar, the rest of the lads were nursing their drinks. Keith smirked and nudged Bruce. "They should be just about parting Steve's cheeks right now."

Bruce laughed, swirling his pint. "Why? Did you tip off security?"

Keith grinned like a cat that got the cream. "Thought it'd be funny to send a little message."

The whole table erupted into laughter. After what felt like an eternity, a flustered and slightly red-faced Steve finally shuffled into the bar, rejoining the group.

"Right, what the hell happened in there?" Bruce asked, barely containing his grin. Steve groaned.

"Let's just say… the 'tip-off' was real. And it wasn't about smuggling. More like… personal hygiene concerns."

The boys burst out laughing again as Steve sank into his chair, relieved to be back where the biggest worry was the price of the next round.

"Right boys, they're calling our flight. Onward!" said Bruce leading them like a boy scout troupe.

The boarding call echoed through the gate area. The lads stepped forward in a loose pack, no luggage to juggle—everything was already checked in and sent ahead.

Steve nudged Bruce as they approached the plane. "So, Bruce, I've only ever been to Benidorm once. Think this trip'll be different?"

Bruce grinned. "Different? Mate, this'll blow Benidorm out of the water."

Steve looked around nervously and lowered his voice. "Can I sit next to you? Flying freaks me out a bit."

Bruce gave him a mock-serious look. "Of course, my little soldier. You won't be flying solo on this one."

Steve's tension eased as they boarded side by side. "Thanks, Bruce. Feels better already."

Bruce clapped him on the back. "Good. Now buckle up. This trip's gonna be one for the books."

The flight attendants glided down the aisle with their trays of drinks and meals. Steve, John, and the others were settling in, some sipping their drinks, others chatting quietly. At the back near the toilets, Bruce struck up a conversation with a pretty flight attendant. She smiled warmly as she approached.

"First time flying with Middle Star Airlines?" she asked, her eyes twinkling.

Bruce grinned, shaking his head. "Nope. This is my first time ever going to the Middle East."

She gave him a playful wink. "Excellent," she said, "then you're in for a treat."

Bruce chuckled and made his way back to his seat. "Boys, you won't believe it," he announced with a cheeky grin as he sat down. "We're not even halfway through the flight, and I've already pulled."

The others burst out laughing, some giving him mock applause while Steve shook his head in disbelief. As the flight attendants wheeled the trolley past, meals were handed out one by one.

"What the hell is this?" Steve asked, poking suspiciously at a tray of something beige and lumpy.

"That's chicken curry, apparently," said Danny, inspecting his with the caution of a man defusing a bomb. "Smells more like someone's armpit on a humid day."

Bruce opened his foil lid and gave it a sniff. "Lads, mine's beef. Or at least it was once. Possibly in the 1980s."

"Do they still serve peanuts?" asked Eric, rummaging through the tray like he'd lost a contact lens.

"Only to people who don't pretend they're on a retreat in Wales," John shot back.

The mini screens on the seat backs flickered to life. The film choice was limited, most nobody had heard of — the best choice, a low-budget action flick starring someone who looked vaguely like Jason Statham's cousin.

"Oh good," said Steve, adjusting his screen. "I've always wanted to see Exploding Cargo 4."

Bruce leaned in. "Watch this bit — he crashes a helicopter with a frying pan and raw determination."

Steve nodded seriously. "Art."

Moments later, Bruce pulled his blanket up, turned to Steve, and said, "If I start snoring or say something rude in my sleep, just jab me."

Steve looked at him. "Mate, if you say something rude in your sleep it'll be the most normal thing you've said all day."

That got a round of chuckles as the cabin lights dimmed slightly, the trays were cleared, and a few of them started drifting off — except for Bruce, who was still scanning the aisle in case his flight attendant came back.

After a few more hours of mild turbulence, lukewarm tea, and questionable film choices, the captain's voice crackled over the intercom.

"Ladies and gentlemen, we'll be commencing our descent into Dubai shortly. Cabin crew, prepare the cabin for landing."

Bruce stirred from a light nap and stretched. "Right, lads — tray tables up, seats back to upright, dignity optional."

There was a shuffle of movement as the group complied — trays snapped closed, seats whirred forward, and Steve, half-asleep, accidentally kneed the man in front of him.

"Sorry, pal," he mumbled, not sounding sorry at all.
The plane touched down with a bump, the familiar chorus of seatbelts clicking undone erupting the second the wheels hit the tarmac.

Bruce stood up too early and got a firm tap on the shoulder from a flight attendant. "Please remain seated until the aircraft comes to a complete stop."

He grinned. "Force of habit, love — I was born impatient."

Once off the plane, the group shuffled through the bright, cavernous corridors of Dubai International. Bruce squinted at a sign, then checked his phone.

"Right, A17. Two-hour layover — let's get through security before one of us ends up detained again. Steve, don't flash your ankles, they might think you're soliciting."

"I was frisked, Bruce. Frisked. I still feel violated."

"Let's hope it isn't the only action you get this trip" said Bernard with a smile, slipping his Gucci sunglasses on.

As they queued at the security checkpoint, Bruce typed a quick message to Josh.

BRUCE: "We've landed — heading to A17 now. You here yet?" Seconds later, a reply pinged back.

JOSH: "In the first-class lounge, mate. Just had a Kobe steak, and a fabulous glass of Shiraz. I'll slum it with you lot at the gate in 45."

Bruce looked up from his phone. "Josh is already here. First-class lounge. Steak, wine, feet probably up on a pillow. Naturally, how the other half live!"

Steve scoffed. "Of course he is. I'm lucky if I get a Pret sandwich and he's eating a cow flown in from Japan."

Eric, still looking nervously over his shoulder, muttered, "Let's just hope Bev hasn't tracked us through the Middle Star app, or something. She's got ways, boys."

John chuckled. "Mate, if she turns up in Phuket with a flip-flop and a grudge, we're not helping you."

The lads made their way toward the gate, chatting, laughing, and adjusting their neck pillows with varying degrees of confidence and fashion sense.

As they stood around Gate A17, leaning on their trolleys and sipping overpriced airport coffees, the WhatsApp group buzzed with a new message.

STU: At the airport now boys. Be prepared for a decent thrashing — I've been practicing.

Steve groaned loud enough for half the terminal to hear. "Oh shite. Stu's been practicing. That's it — I'm out."

Danny laughed. "You were never in, mate. Last time you hit a drive it nearly killed a dog on the next fairway."

Steve scowled. "He could already beat us all with one hand. I'm thinking of going scuba diving instead."

Bruce raised an eyebrow. "You can't swim."

"True," Steve shrugged. "But drowning still sounds easier than trying to beat Stu at golf."

The lads chuckled as Bruce glanced up and spotted a figure approaching — tall, tanned, and wheeling the most immaculate hand luggage any of them had ever seen.

"Here he is, lads. Mr Bloody Flash," Bruce muttered.

"Look at that Louis Vuitton bag," Danny added. "Probably cost more than my car."

Josh grinned as he strolled up to the group. "Hope it wasn't too rough for you boys back in cattle class."

Steve gave a solemn nod. "Oh, it was a dream. Though at least Bruce managed to pull a flight attendant."

Josh smirked. "Nice, still got it then Brucie."

"Never lost it old lad, never lost it!" replied Bruce

Just then, the boarding call echoed through the terminal.
As they approached the gate, Josh clapped Bruce on the shoulder and said with a grin, "I'm heading left. See you in Phuket." And with that, he disappeared into the First-Class queue.

Chapter Five

Welcome to Paradise

The second leg of the flight was mercifully smooth — no turbulence, no delays, and no one arrested mid-air. Most of the lads dozed or watched films, while Josh, seated comfortably up in First Class, made very good use of the drinks list. By the time they landed in Phuket, he was looking suspiciously cheerful, having polished off several glasses of a particularly rare 50-year-old cognac.

"I think I just drank a year's rent for my offices in Dubai," he declared, swaying slightly as they stepped off the plane into hot and thick, humid afternoon.

The tropical heat hit like a wall, sticky and immediate, as they made their way toward immigration. Followed by a near sub-zero aircon blowing inside the terminal. And naturally, things started going wrong almost instantly for Steve. Once through immigration, the headed to the bag carousel.

"Sir, step this way," an officer said, blocking Steve's path.

Steve blinked. "Me? What for?" The officer didn't answer, just motioned for him to follow. The rest of the group paused to watch him being escorted to a secondary screening area.

"You've got to be kidding me," Steve groaned as another officer began unzipping his bags.

"Empty everything, please."

Bruce leaned over to Danny. "Bet it's the Wotsits."

Danny smirked. "Or that suspicious packet of ginger nuts Gloria packed for him."

Steve, now red in the face, held up a single flip-flop. "What exactly are you expecting to find in here, mate? A smuggled pineapple?"

"I'd like you to be patient sir, this hopefully won't take long. But the more you argue, the longer it will take" said the customs officer as he looked at the contents.

Meanwhile, over at the baggage carousel, Eric was pacing like a man about to deliver twins.

"Where's my bag?" he snapped. "The clubs are here, but no suitcase."

He stormed over to the airline help desk, where a smiling Thai lady calmly checked the records.

"Ah yes, Mr Eric," she said with a smile. "Your bag is… still in Dubai. Very sorry."

"You what?" Eric replied.

"It will arrive tomorrow evening. We deliver to your hotel, no problem."

Eric looked like he might combust. "So, what am I meant to wear until then, I've had the same clothes on since yesterday?"

The woman's smile widened. "You have an allowance to buy some clothes, the markets are very cheap?"

Eric exhaled slowly. Luckily, I have some golf clothes in my carry-on.

Brilliant. You'll be the only man in Phuket in a Gogo bar in plus fours and a visor." Shouted Bruce.

John walked over, grinning. "Look on the bright side — at least your underwear is having its own little break. Probably sipping a cocktail somewhere."

As the last of the group cleared customs — including a flustered and deeply offended Steve, muttering about "state-sanctioned rummaging, and again "looking up my arse!"

Bernard looking over said to Steve "What bad luck mate, having a colonoscopy in the UK, and Thailand. And you haven't left the airport yet. You must be well lubed up now and ready to hit Bangla straight away!" The group burst out laughing, Steve simply shook his head.

They regrouped near the exit. "Right, everyone accounted for?" asked Bruce.

"Just about," Eric grumbled. "All of me except my dignity and wardrobe."

"Good," Bruce replied, already fishing out his phone. "I'll message Stu — he should be in the hotel by now."

As they waited, Josh walked passed with a porter in tow.
"I have a car waiting, I'm heading to my hotel, The luxury resort of Amanpati, send me a message later Bruce for the meet up.

A few minutes later, their own hotel rep arrived — a young Thai man with a clipboard, a grin, and a badge that read Mr Pong. He ticked off their names, loaded the clubs and battered suitcases onto a trolley, and waved them toward a waiting minibus with cold bottled water in the holders and blessed air conditioning.

They packed into the back, some with knees awkwardly pressed against their bags, and with a cheery thumbs-up from Mr Pong, the bus rolled out of the airport and onto the road to Patong. As they made their way through the winding streets, the scenery slowly changed — from highways lined with palm trees to the bustling chaos of scooters, tuk-tuks, and neon signs. Then, as they entered Patong proper, the strip lit up in full, exotic glory. Massage parlours seemed to line every inch of the road, each one brighter, more colourful, and more outrageous than the last. Women in matching uniforms waved eagerly from doorways, some blowing kisses, others holding up laminated menus of "services" with suspiciously ambiguous wording.

Eric's face lit up like a kid in a candy shop. He pressed his nose to the glass.

"There are so many massage shops here, even I might finally relax… maybe even forget about Bev!" he shouted over the noise.

"You'll forget your name by the time we've done two rounds of tequila, and had your dangly bits tickled" Bruce shot back.

"I've already forgotten your name," muttered Steve, pretending to nod off against the window.

Laughter filled the minibus as they swerved around another tuk-tuk and caught sight of Patong Beach gleaming in the late afternoon sun. It was loud, sweaty, and gloriously chaotic.

"Right lads," said Bruce. "Welcome to paradise you perverts. You are lucky, lucky boys." The whole bus erupted in cheers.

The bus veered down a narrow street, dodging mopeds like a slalom course, and finally pulled into a leafy driveway framed by palms and bougainvillaea. A large wooden sign carved with gold leaf read The Royal Orchid Resort – Patong. Beneath it, in smaller lettering: Where Your Dreams Begin...

"Sounds promising," muttered Danny, eyeing a couple in swimwear sipping cocktails by the entrance.

The boys piled out of the minibus, stretching backs and cracking knees like a team of pensioners. Mr. Pong had already summoned a small army of bellboys to offload the clubs and bags. The smell of lemongrass and distant grilling meat wafted through the air.

At the reception desk, a smiling hostess handed them all cold towels and a welcome drink that tasted vaguely of pineapple and rocket fuel.

"I could get used to this," said Eric, knocking his back in one gulp.
"That's the spirit," said Bruce, before leaning over the counter. "nine rooms, all booked under Bruce Howard. And I assume the presidential suite has a bidet and a personal masseuse?"

The receptionist blinked, unsure whether to laugh. "All rooms have a rain shower and daily housekeeping, Mr. Howard."

"Close enough," he said, tossing his passport on the counter.

"Excuse me," said Craig. Do you have a spa where I can get a manicure, my nails are awful".

"Certainly sir, details are in the brochures in your rooms" she replied.

"Have you turned gay all of a sudden" Danny asked, with a puzzled look "Manicures, flipin heck!"

Room keys distributed and baggage assigned, the boys regrouped in the lobby.

Rory said grinning. "We're here. Now the holiday starts."

"Agreed," Bruce nodded. "Dump the bags. Meet by the pool in 30. First rounds on me."

"And by 'round' you mean——?" asked Danny.

Bruce grinned. "Buckets. With straws. Welcome to Thailand." As the group filed toward the lifts, Eric turned back and glanced out at the Patong skyline, now glowing pink in the sunset.

"Honestly," he muttered to himself, "this might just be the trip that saves me from therapy. I'll just pop out to that market opposite and get some clothes for tonight"

The elevator pinged. eight men on a mission disappeared into the resort. Thirty minutes later, the lads began to filter out to the pool in various states of tropical unpreparedness. Bruce was first down, already halfway through his second coconut cocktail. He sprawled on a lounger in Union Jack swim shorts that left little to the imagination, aviators reflecting the turquoise pool, looking perfectly at ease—until he spotted a familiar figure.

"Bloody hell," he muttered, shielding his eyes.

There, lying poolside with the calm confidence of someone who'd arrived hours ago and already done yoga, was Stu. His gleaming bald head caught the sun like a polished cue ball, offset by a pair of designer shades and an immaculate white polo. He sipped something tall and green, looking every bit the man who knew exactly where the best seat in the hotel was.

Bruce walked over, arms wide. "Here he is! Mr. Single-Figure Handicap himself."

Stu stood up, a towering man, well over 6 foot 6, flashing a grin, and gave Bruce a solid handshake-hug combo. "Welcome to paradise, Brewster, pool's warm, and I've already been offered a boat trip, a motorbike, and someone's sister, and I've only been here four hours."

Bruce laughed. "What about a hat for that shiny dome of yours?"

"I'm letting the scalp breathe," Stu said, striking a majestic pose. "Besides, I haven't burned it since Ayia Napa '03."

Bruce settled into the lounger next to him, chuckling. "Class." A few moments later, the others began arriving in full holiday disarray.

Keith clomped out with flip-flops on the wrong feet and "Ibiza 2004" board shorts that had seen better decades. He was already turning a slight lobster pink across the shoulders despite having applied sun cream like masonry paint. Danny strolled out in a tiger singlet and cargo shorts, sipping something fluorescent from a hollowed-out pineapple. Then came Eric. Wearing a tight 7-Eleven T-shirt and Muay Thai shorts with gold dragons up the sides, he marched across the tiles like a man with nothing to lose.

"Well, lads, what do we think?" he called out, arms wide. "New country, new me!"

"You look like a kids' TV presenter who's had a breakdown, what happened to the plus fours?" Steve said flatly.

"Sun cream leaked all over the gear, Anyway, I feel relaxed already," Eric replied. "I reckon after a few of those Thai massages I'll even forget about Bev."

"You sure you want one of those massages?" Bruce smirked. "Some of them come with a surprise ending."

Steve said with a puzzled look. "I thought it was called a happy ending, that sounds frightening"

"You seem to be well informed Steve" Said Bruce as he laid back on his lounger.

Stu raised an eyebrow. "Careful. You'll end up in a documentary." Laughter rippled through the group as a waiter arrived with a metal bucket of ice-cold local beers.

"To forgetting Bev," said Eric, grabbing one.
"To surviving the flight," Steve added.
"To surviving what's coming next," Bruce grinned. "We've got seafood booked tonight… and I've already marked out a few massage joints on Google. But the real action start when we hit The Koala Bar, that's where the action is boys!"

Danny looked out toward the road. "There's hundreds of them out there, all offering to massage us. Feels like every other shop's offering a rub and a grin."

Eric perked up. "I saw one called Sawatdee Knead You. I don't know what that means, but it's calling me."

"Just don't end up in Very Regretful Prison," Stu deadpanned.

The laughter carried into the golden hour as the sun dipped behind the palm trees, and the Bluetooth speaker kicked into a reggae version of 'Sweet Child o' Mine'. Bruce leaned back, stretched, and smiled. This was exactly the chaos they needed

Chapter Six

Opening Nights Carnage

The sun had just dipped below the horizon, casting a soft amber glow over the rooftops of Patong. In their rooms, the boys were preparing for what Bruce had ominously called "an exploratory mission."

Bernard stood at the mirror, eyeing himself like a man auditioning for a 70s comeback tour, yet in his mind, he thought he was the character from Top Gun in the 80s. He popped open the third button of his satin shirt, then the fourth. His chest, generously carpeted and proudly sunbed tanned, gleamed under the hotel lighting. Hanging in the middle of it all was a chunky gold medallion that caught the light and spun like a hypnotist's watch.

He gave himself a wink. "Bernie's on the prowl tonight, you lucky ladies" he said with a grin, fishing a little blue pill from the drawer and sliding it into his wallet like a secret weapon. "Locked, loaded, and ready to face the enemy."

Down the hall, Eric was hunched over the sink, locked in battle with his hair using a flimsy hotel comb and what he thought was hair gel—hastily bought that afternoon from 7-Eleven after his luggage went AWOL. He squeezed out a generous glob, slapped it through his fringe, and paused as a strong minty scent wafted up.

"Smells fresh, this gel," he muttered approvingly. "Tingly." Then the tingle turned to burn. Then to full-blown ice storm. Frowning, he picked up the tube and squinted at the label. Mostly Thai script, unreadable—but in tiny English below the logo: Toothpaste. He stared into the mirror. His hair now stood tall, glossy, and aggressively mint-scented. Still in his now slightly sweaty 7-Eleven t-shirt and Thai boxing shorts, he glanced again at himself in the mirror and nodded.

"That'll work." And with that, Eric strutted out of the bathroom like a man who had no regrets—and no luggage.

Danny, meanwhile, was trimming his nose hairs with the nail scissors he found in the free toiletries bag. "Nothing says ready for action like good grooming," he muttered, lips pursed with concentration.

Steve had ironed a shirt, then got bored and crumpled it again attempting a TikTok dance he insisted he could still remember from lockdown. He eventually gave up and went for a black polo and jeans, texting the group chat: "Ready for lift-off, gentlemen."

Bruce was the first in the lobby, dressed in a short-sleeved linen shirt, fake aviators hanging from the open neck, and flip-flops that made a slap with every step. One by one, the rest of the lads drifted down — some sharp, some already resembling the morning after.

Then came Stu, walking in looking like a retired Bond villain on vacation—crisp white polo, tailored shorts, and the smug swagger of a man who'd already won the golf before breakfast.

"Go easy, lads," he warned as they assembled around him. "We're on the tee at 11 tomorrow."

Bruce laughed, throwing an arm around his shoulder. "It's just one or two, mate. You know, cultural integration and all that."

"I know exactly the type of cultural integrating you are thinking of my debauched friend," Stu muttered.

"I do bloody hope so" Bruce replied winking at Stu, and laughed out loud.

"Right lads, change of plan. Cancel the seafood, it's too much interference with our drinking" announced Bruce.

Outside, the balmy night wrapped around them like a velvet cloak as they piled into tuk-tuks and bounced along the road toward Bangla. The street pulsed with neon: bars thumping music, hawkers selling wristbands and fake Ray-Bans, and girls outside massage shops in sexy little shorts shouting "Massage, handsome boys". They replied with a loud cheer and a wave.

As they rolled to a stop near the entrance to Bangla Road main entrance, The big banner across the street read Patong Beach Phuket Thailand. Bruce turned around and clapped his hands. "Right, gentlemen. Phones on silent. Wallets in front pockets. Dignity optional. Let the opening night of carnage commence!"

Bars lined the streets, one after another, fluorescent lights flickering over smiling women perched on stools like meerkats, middle-aged men sat drinking beers and chatting to beautiful ladies. Men and women in the streets holding signs for ping pong shows, and cheap drinks.

"Chang sir? Leo, we have all beers. You handsome!" as a young Thai lady grabbed Eric's arm. "Your shorts, oh sexy boy" she finished as they walked faster passed the bar.

"Only thing that'll be rubbed out of you is your wallet," Bernard said, laughing, his medallion bouncing proudly on his chest.

Steve leaned out the side and shouted, "I think one of them just proposed to me!"

Danny replied, "She's got good taste, then. Or poor vision, but really proposed to your wallet, mate!"

And with that, they stepped into the blaze of lights and sound, a line of middle-aged mischief-makers, ready to make memories they probably wouldn't remember. The street was alive — a carnival of chaos. Music pounded from every direction, lights strobed in epileptic defiance of taste, and the smell of grilled meat, motorbike fumes, street drains, and cheap perfume collided in the humid air.

They didn't so much walk as get swept along in the Bangla tide, shoulder to shoulder with tourists, touts, and the occasional wandering ladyboy who gave Bernard a wink that he pretended not to see — but definitely clocked. Their first stop was The Koala Bar, where Bruce was greeted like royalty and a Change beer tower appeared before they'd even ordered.

"G'day, boys!" called the owner, a leathery Aussie with a voice like a gravel road and the belly of a man who hadn't seen a vegetable since 1997. "Happy hour goes all bloody night if you're drinking fast enough!"

They laughed, cheered, and took seats around two sticky wooden tables.

And that's when Pete appeared. Sunburned, beaming, and possibly semi-retired from reality, Pete was wearing mirrored sunglasses despite it being fully dark, and a vest that read NO WIFI, NO WORRIES, NO WOMEN – NO THANKS.

"Brucie, ya bloody legend!" he hollered, bear-hugging him with all the enthusiasm of a man who had already downed four buckets of something toxic.

"Pete, you old reprobate!" Bruce grinned, clapping him on the back. "Boys, meet Pete. Came here for a week ten years ago, hasn't sobered up since."

Pete saluted the group, took one look at Bernard's shirtless-and-swinging ensemble, and laughed. "Mate, did you lose your dignity before check-in, or is that optional with the room key?"

Bernard flexed his chest and let his gold medallion catch the light like a disco ball. "This," he said solemnly, "is the look of confidence. And mild chest burn."

They were halfway through the second beer tower when Pete leaned in with a glint in his eye.

"You boys want something special for your first night? A little... cultural deep dive?"

"Oh Christ," said Stu, already regretting everything.

Pete ignored him. "I'm talkin' Nanny Wong's. Big and bold, and all happens behind a thick curtain on the door. No photos inside. Place has the best drinks, worst decisions, and a show that'll either make you laugh, cry, or change your orientation."

Eric leaned forward, eyes wide. "What kind of show are we talking?"

Pete just grinned. "You'll know it when you see it."

Steve looked uncertain. "Is this like that bar in Pattaya where a bloke pulled a goldfish out of somewhere a goldfish shouldn't be?"

Pete chuckled, completely serious. "No animals. Just ambition."

Bernard stood, raising his beer. "To Nanny Wong's. And to whatever mysterious magic lies within!"

Bruce drained his glass. "Alright lads, into the abyss."

As they spilled out of the bar and onto the street again, the night swallowed them whole. Neon signs blinked. Tuk-tuks growled past. And a woman in six-inch heels tried to convince Danny she was previous winner of Miss Thailand, though he remained unconvinced — especially as she adjusted her voice mid-sentence.

They walked, they joked, they dodged offers of "good price!" massages and ping-pong flyers with photos that defied physics. And finally, down a narrow alley, Pete stopped beside a neon extravaganza.

"This is it," he said, nodding at the bouncers and through a very, very thick curtain.

The door opened. A woman in a red cheongsam dress, and ten tonnes of eyeliner greeted them with a smile that could cut glass.

"Welcome, boys," she purred. "You're just in time for the fire show."

Eric blinked. "What kind of fire…?"

But they were already being ushered inside, laughter trailing behind them like perfume. The door closed. The street outside kept roaring. And inside, the real madness was just beginning.

From Nanny Wong's steamy little foyer, they were ushered through a beaded curtain into the main bar — and it was like walking into the belly of a neon-lit jungle. The central stage pulsed with coloured lights, and four girls in tiny sequin outfits danced in slow, hypnotic synchrony to a remix of Thai techno music that didn't quite match the tempo or the mood. Two at each end of the stage, dressed exactly as they were when they were born!

"I feel like we've stepped into a fever dream," muttered Bruce, looking around as the group settled on seats around the central stage.

A waitress, dressed in a revealing mini skirt and top, with a blue neon badge reading Lilly dropped off a round of Beers — and handed over the bill with a dramatic flourish.

Bruce blinked at it. "Fourteen quid a drink! Is there gold in it?" "No, just regret," Stu said, eyeing his blue cocktail suspiciously. "And maybe some antifreeze."

Before Steve could even lift his beer, a petite Thai woman bent down from the stage holding what looked like a metre-long piece of foam pipe insulation. She smiled sweetly, blew a kiss, and without a word — whack! — brought it down across his back with surprising speed and precision, not once, not twice but in a frenzied action.

Steve yelped like a kicked puppy and twisted in his seat, startled. "MUMMY!" he squealed, arms flailing.

That was it. The boys erupted in a chorus of laughter. Danny had tears streaming down his face. "Oh my god... Steve just went full childhood trauma!"

Bruce banged the table. "I've never heard a grown man scream like that."

Even the dancer on stage paused mid-pivot and looked over with a grin. The woman hit Steve again, a quick tap this time, then gave a little bow and walked off, twirling the foam baton like she was heading to the Olympics.

"I don't even know what that was," Steve said, hunched slightly.

"Some kind of spa therapy," Eric offered. "Except instead of oils and relaxation, you get assaulted with plumbing materials."

She then turned and place her buttocks about 3 inches from Steve's nose, gesturing for him to spank her with the pipe. But before Steve could move, Bernard was already spanking the hell out of her, whilst sweating like a man on a mission.

"She likes you," Bruce said, taking a big swig of his beer.

"I need a lie down," Steve muttered.

"You're not getting one," Bruce grinned. "You're getting another round. And a front-row seat to something you've never seen before."

As more girls came on stage and the tempo picked up, the madness of Nanny Wong's tightened its grip. The music got louder, the lights flickered faster, and the drinks kept coming. It was absurd, it was expensive, it was slightly dangerous — and it was only their first proper night in Phuket.

And somewhere deep in the chaos, Bernard raised his glass and declared, "Lads — we're alive, and it's only Sunday!"
They all cheered. It was going to be a long, beautiful week.
Jet lag started to kick in, mingling perfectly with the steady stream of alcohol they'd been ingesting for hours. Their swagger out of Nanny Wong's was less rockstar and more newly born deer.

"Lads," slurred Bruce, waving his arm in the air like a shepherd herding tired livestock. "Time for bed. Golf tomorrow. We need to hydrate… with cheese."

Instead of heading straight for the hotel, Bruce veered off down a side street. The others followed, bleary-eyed and floppy-limbed, unsure if this was another bar or if Bruce had finally lost the plot. But then it appeared — the sacred glow of Thailand's most hallowed ground: 7-Eleven. As the automatic door opened, that famous bing-bong chime rang out, echoing through the fluorescent-lit haven like a beacon of comfort.

"Yes!" Bruce shouted over his shoulder. "There it is! The sound of champions."

They stumbled inside, greeted by icy air-con and rows of snacks, mystery meat sticks, and neon-coloured drinks.

"You have to get one of these cheese toasties," Bruce announced like a man preaching gospel. "They're fabulous. They cost seventy pence.

It's basically a crime not to buy one." He grabbed two from the fridge and turned back to the group, eyes shining. "This is the real Thailand."

Eric blinked at the selection. "Is it just me, or do these sandwiches have fillings I've never heard of?"

"That's the charm!" Bruce laughed. "mystery perfection."

Danny held up a seaweed-flavoured Lay's packet, frowned, then put it back like it had offended him. Steve was studying a freezer full of what looked like fluorescent green ice lollies with suspicion.

Bernard, meanwhile, was already unwrapping a sausage skewer. "This tastes like heaven, certainly beats the burger vans of the 80s after the clubs in Doncaster" he said, chewing, "and I respect that."

After a few minutes of chaotic snacking and drunken purchases — including a durian cake no one wanted, and a tiny fan Steve claimed he "needed for his face" — the toasties were ready, and they finally made their way back to the hotel.

The streets were quieter now, with only the odd scooter zipping past and the hum of late-night music in the distance. Patong was slowly powering down, but the lads were barely holding on to their own battery life. By the time they reached the lobby, silence had replaced the earlier roar of jokes and bravado. They nodded at the dozing security guard, squeezed into the lift, and rode up in exhausted silence. As they each peeled off to their rooms, Bruce gave one last toastie-laden salute.

"Rest up, lads. Tomorrow, we golf, bus leaves at 10.00. And if anyone throws up on the 5th hole, you're paying for drinks all night."

No one replied. The only sound was the ding of the lift doors closing, and the faint crinkle of plastic-wrapped cheese toasties.

Chapter Seven

The Hangover Handicap

The room was dark, quiet — and then the phone rang. "Good morning, Mr. Howard, this is your 8:30 alarm call," said a far-too-cheerful voice from reception.

Bruce groaned, one eye creaking open. His head was pounding like a bass drum at Glastonbury. He reached blindly for the nightstand, knocked over a bottle of water, then finally found the two Paracetamols he'd stashed in readiness. Down they went with a half gulp of lukewarm beer from the night before, and a bottle of M-150, the Thai energy drink of champions, hitting his taste buds like a thousand volts! — medicinal, he told himself.

Staggering to the bathroom, he muttered something that sounded like "never drinking again" and stepped into the shower. The instant cold blast made him yelp. "Oh God," he groaned, clutching his head. "My head feels like I've been hit by a tuk-tuk."

Across the corridor, Stu was a vision of smug efficiency. Already dressed in a crisp polo shirt and khaki shorts, he sat on his balcony, sipping a perfectly brewed coffee while strolling through his phone. He'd taken notes on Red Canyon Country Club — wind direction, bunker placements, green speeds. It was all neatly categorised, colour-coded, and possibly laminated. He glanced out at the bright Phuket morning.

"Let the games begin," he murmured with a smirk.

Meanwhile, Eric looked like a crime scene. He was still sprawled across his bed in his Thai boxing shorts and an oversized 7-Eleven t-shirt. His chest rose and fell slowly beneath a blanket of crushed crisps. A half-eaten cheese toastie was stuck to his thigh. He snored like a man with no regrets and zero intention of waking up before noon.

Down the hall, Steve's alarm went off with a robotic buzz that matched the feeling in his skull. He blinked blearily, grabbed his phone, and groaned. "What fresh hell is this?"

Dragging himself upright, he shuffled toward the bathroom. "Everything hurts," he muttered, stripping off like a moulting lizard. "Even my eyelashes."

In the next room, Rory was already in the shower — and not quietly. "I've got the hangover from hell!" he yelled to no one. "Who let me have sambuca? I hate sambuca!"

Downstairs in the breakfast room, the survivors were slowly assembling. Bernard sat in sunglasses, chewing dry toast like it was cardboard. Danny nursed a cup of black coffee and stared into the abyss. Even Bruce, freshly showered but visibly wilting, looked like he was running on fumes and fumes alone. Then the doors parted and in walked Craig — an explosion of colour and enthusiasm. His shorts were neon green, his polo shirt featured pineapples playing golf, and his visor was tilted just enough to be ironically cool.

"Morning boys!" he beamed. "What a day to rip up a golf course!" He clapped Bruce on the back. Bruce winced. "Ready to hit the first tee?"

Bruce blinked slowly. "I'm ready to hit something. Just not sure it'll be a golf ball. Mate, come on, what the hell are you wearing. You look like Timmy Mallet on a bad wash day, do you have a mirror in your room?"

"You simply don't appreciate style Bruce" replied Craig.

Stu strolled in, still looking like a man in control of his own destiny. "Tee times at eleven, lads. Plenty of time for regrets and rehydration. Let's make this respectable, shall we?"

Eric stumbled in, looking like he'd been recently dug up. "Has anyone seen my toastie?" he asked, deadpan. "I think I lost it in the bed sheets." The lads stared at him.

"I'm still eating it," he added with a shrug.

They all laughed — some through the pain — and one by one, they pulled themselves together, grabbed their clubs, and headed out for Day One of the Phuket Golf Classic. What could possibly go wrong?

The mini bus idled outside the resort, waiting to transport the half-dead crew to their first round at Red Canyon. Craig bounded in first, still bursting with enthusiasm. Stu followed with military efficiency, double-checking tee times and making sure everyone's clubs were loaded. One by one, the rest of the lads stumbled into the minibus like zombies heading for battle. Eric clutched a bottle of Lucozade like it was holy water. Bernard adjusted his golf cap with shaky hands. Rory groaned as he slid into a seat and immediately passed out.

Just as the minibus door slid shut with a soft thunk, Bruce leaned back in his seat and shouted cheerfully, "Sabai, Sabai, krap!" It was a phrase he'd picked up from the smiling tour guide at the airport — Thai for relaxed and comfortable, and it seemed like the perfect motto for the week ahead.

As the driver pulled away, Bruce's phone pinged with a message.

Josh: See you there, boys. Hope you've brought your A-game. I've just birdied the omelette station. Laughter rippled through the group.

"Smug bastard," Bruce muttered with a grin, typing back Let's see if you're still smiling after the 3rd hole.

As the minibus rolled out through the hotel gates, silence fell. One by one, heads lolled against windows. The air-conditioning purred, and for the next thirty minutes, the road hummed beneath them as everyone dozed in various states of denial about how much they drank the night before. The Red Canyon Country Club came into view — a lush, sprawling course perched on the coast, manicured within an inch of paradise. The greens sparkled. The fairways rolled like velvet hills. And the sun beat down gently, promising both glory and sunburn in equal measure.

The bus pulled up at the bag drop area, where a small battalion of caddies — all female, dressed in matching pastel polos and logo-emblazoned baseball caps — stood ready. In an instant, the rear doors swung open, and the women moved like clockwork, collecting golf bags with practiced ease.

"Here we go," muttered Bernard, stepping out and stretching with a wince. "Time to ruin a good walk."

Bruce handed his clubs over and turned to thank the approaching caddie — and then paused.

Her name badge read simply: Kitti Porn. Bruce blinked. "Okay lads, I'm sorted. Found my caddie," he said, grinning. "I love your name."

The young woman smiled without missing a beat.

"Sir, if I had one hundred baht for every time a farang made fun of my name," she said in perfect English, "I'd be very rich and retired by now."

The lads laughed, and Bruce raised his hands in mock surrender. "Sorry, just joking. Don't mind me. I'm Bruce. Let's have a great game." She gave him a playful nod. "Don't worry, Bruce. I'll keep you out of the bunkers and away from bad jokes."

Eric elbowed Bruce as they walked toward the clubhouse. "You've already found your soulmate, Brucie boy. A woman who can take the piss out of you before the first tee."

Bruce grinned. "This is going to be a good day, mate. This is better than dark grey Yorkshire golf clubs!"

They filed in to check in, found their carts, and got ready to tee off. Red Canyon was waiting… and so was the chaos that usually followed this crew wherever they went.

As they milled around the first tee, there was a sudden hush among the group as Eric strutted out of the pro shop, looking like a man reborn.

"Bloody hell," said Steve, shielding his eyes. "Who's this fashion icon?"

Eric beamed. He was decked out head-to-toe in a crisp, brand-new golfing outfit from the club shop — fresh polo shirt, tailored shorts, white cap, and gleaming shoes. Even his glove looked like it had been custom-stitched.

"Thought I'd make an effort," Eric said, doing a small twirl. "Figured it was time I looked like a golfer, even if I can't play like one."

"Cleanest he's looked since we landed," Danny muttered. "You plan on playing or modelling today?"

Eric grinned. "Both. I'm available for autographs at the turn." Bruce clapped his hands together.

"Right, lads. Before the week gets too messy and we're all too sunburnt or hungover to stand straight — let's have a team photo." The group groaned, adjusted hats, tugged shirts into place, and gathered reluctantly.

"Come on," Bruce said. "It'll be a collector's item. Twelve idiots on tour. Someone's gotta document this before the lawsuits roll in." He waved over one of the caddies. "Kitti, would you mind taking a few photos of this rabble?"

Kitti smiled warmly and took the phone. "Of course, Mr Bruce. Everyone, say… birdie!"

"Breathe in you fat bastards," Shouted Pete. So it was, twelve friends from across the world, each with wildly different fashion choices and levels of sobriety, lined up on the first tee of Red Canyon Country Club — ready to begin their week-long golfing battle. With their clubs at their sides and the Thai sun gleaming off sunglasses and bald patches, they looked less like professional athletes and more like a police line-up for a particularly stylish midlife crime spree.

"Perfect," Kitti said, snapping a few shots from different angles. "Very handsome. Very… energetic, and very sexy."

"Energetic?" Steve muttered. "I can barely stand."

Bruce patted him on the back. "Good. That means you're loose."

Stu checked his watch and nodded. "Let's get started. It's 11:00 on the dot." With that, the first group teed up. Sun high, fairways open, caddies smiling — and twelve hopeful swings ahead.

Stu stepped up first, teeing his ball with the precision of a man who'd been rehearsing this moment all winter.

"Best of luck gentlemen, you'll need it!" He said with a grin. He then took a couple of smooth practice swings, then unleashed a beautifully crisp drive that drew gently into the middle of the fairway, landing with a satisfying bounce around the 300-yard mark. He turned to the others with a grin. " There you go, you rabble — that's your marker."

Next up was Craig. Effortless swing. Solid contact. The ball soared, climbing high before flattening out and sailing past Stu's drive by a good twenty yards.

"You've got a game on your hands now, boyo," Bernard said with a grin, elbowing Stu, who was already slumped in the cart, looking unimpressed.

"It's a long game, boys," Craig said coolly, tossing his tee back in his pocket like a man who'd done this a thousand times. Bruce and John followed — solid efforts, both, each finding the fairway, albeit some seventy yards behind Stu.

"Respectable," Bruce said, straightening up and adjusting his cap. "For men of our vintage."

"Vintage?" John scoffed. "Speak for yourself — I'm still in my prime."

The first hole was already shaping up to be a classic. As the first group rolled off down the fairway, the second fourball stepped up to the tee: Pete, Bernard, Danny, and Rory. Bernard cracked his knuckles theatrically and adjusted his bright red visor.

"Right, let's show those posers ahead how the veterans do it." Pete nodded, lining up. "If by veterans you mean 'bad backs and bold lies,' then yes."

Pete's drive was steady — not long, but straight enough. Bernard followed with a wild swing that sent the ball skimming low, miraculously staying on course before settling near a tree. "I'm calling that a stinger," he said with a wink.

Danny's shot wasn't much better — a wicked slice that barely stayed in bounds. "Didn't know we were playing the neighbouring course," Rory joked as he teed up. But Rory surprised them all with a cracking drive, easily the best of the group.

"Alright, now I'm awake," he said, throwing his tee in the air.

Then came the final group: Keith, Josh, Eric, and Steve. Josh, already in rhythm from his omelette-fuelled warmup at the resort, smacked a clean drive down the centre. Keith followed, solid and deliberate. Then Eric stepped up — wearing his freshly purchased pro shop outfit like he was teeing off at The Masters. He took a deep breath, waggled the club like he'd seen on YouTube, then topped the ball so badly it rolled about 20 yards.

"Mate," Steve said, trying to stifle a laugh. "That outfit deserves better."

Eric turned and shrugged. "Fashion over function, boys."

Steve's shot finished the rotation — a decent drive that landed just off the fairway. He nodded to the others.

"Alright. Let's go find out who's walking and who's searching." With that, the final group set off, laughter following them down the first.

The front nine at Red Canyon was as stunning as it was punishing. Sweeping ocean views, palm-lined fairways, and greens slicker than a used car salesman. On the third hole, a par three over water, Danny thinned his shot so badly it skipped across the lake like a flat stone and somehow landed just off the green.

"Shot of the day!" he declared, as if that was the plan all along.

On the fifth, Bernard tried to blast his way out of a bunker but succeeded only in sending sand directly into Rory's mouth.

"Christ, Bernie!" Rory gagged. "I was hoping for a cold drink, not a desert buffet."

Bruce, meanwhile, was playing his usual game — moments of brilliance peppered with chaos. He holed a thirty-foot birdie putt on the 6th, then lost a ball two shots later in a bush he insisted wasn't there on the map. Craig and Stu were locked in an unspoken battle. Every time one striped a drive, the other would quietly nod, then try to outdo it. Stu's 300-yard opener had been topped more than once by Craig's smooth, effortless bombs.

Eric — despite looking the part in his gleaming new golf gear — had swung between flashes of genius and complete collapse. On the 8th, he managed to chip in from off the green and celebrated like he'd just won The Open, raising his arms and nearly falling backwards into the caddie cart.

Finally, the groups began filtering in toward the halfway house at the turn. A shaded wooden hut nestled beside the ninth tee; it was a welcome sight. Cold drinks, salty snacks, and a chance to regroup. Bruce was already on his second Chang beer, leaning against a pillar, sweat-soaked but smiling.

Then Steve appeared, trudging up the path like a man returning from war. His face and arms were beetroot red, his shirt clinging to him, hair plastered to his forehead.

Bruce nearly spat out his drink.

"Fooook sake, Steve — did you forget to put on your factor 50?"

Steve groaned. "Yeah, yeah — I look like the ginger kid who got left outside a Wetherspoons during a Bank Holiday heatwave.

Eric took one look at him and burst out laughing. "Mate, that's going to sting!"

Josh added, "You're only halfway round — by the 18th we'll be spreading mozzarella on you and calling it bruschetta."

Even the caddies giggled behind their visors. Steve slumped onto a bench and reached for a bottle of water. "Laugh it up, lads. But if I survive this round, I'm buying aloe vera by the bucket." His caddie walked over with a chilled towel and placed it on his head.

"Khun Steve, you Ting Tong " she said.

"What does that mean" Steve asked.

"You don't want to know" Pete chimed in.

Bruce clinked his beer bottle against Steve's. "Welcome to Thailand, mate, Gloria would be proud!"

With the sun still beating down and the back nine waiting, the crew took a few moments to hydrate, reapply sunscreen (some more diligently than others), and retell the greatest shots — and worst disasters — of the morning.

Refuelled and slightly revived, Bruce and his fourball — Craig, John, and Stu — began the short walk to the 10th tee, which sat just beyond the halfway house, shaded by tall palms and nestled between two manicured hillsides. Bruce finished the last few gulps of his Chang, let out a satisfied sigh, and casually tossed the empty bottle into the bin.

"Right then," he said to himself, grabbing his driver. "Time to dazzle the gallery."

He gave his club a lazy twirl, then a few loose practice swings that looked more like someone swatting flies. The rest of the lads gathered near the bench by the hut, drinks in hand, watching with the grins of spectators hoping for either brilliance or carnage — either would be entertaining.

Stu stood beside the tee box, calm and composed, sipping a fresh pineapple and mango juice. Not a bead of sweat on him. His shirt was still crisp. His swing would be too.

Steve, on the other hand, had found some relief in the form of a freshly chopped coconut, straw poking out the top like a little umbrella of hope. He slurped noisily and groaned in satisfaction.

"This," he said, holding it up like a trophy, "this is the business."

Bernard leaned over, squinting. "You can't get those in bloody York. Closest I've seen is a coconut-flavoured cider at Morrisons."

The group chuckled as Bruce stepped up to the tee, adjusted his glove, and gave the fairway a wobbly-eyed stare. "Gentlemen, prepare to be inspired," he announced.

Eric called from behind, "We're always inspired by your ability to still walk upright after nine holes and seven beers."

Bruce grinned, lined up… and with a mighty swing, launched his ball into a majestic arc — straight down the middle. It landed with a satisfying bounce and roll.

"BOOM! That's how you do it!" he said, turning and raising both arms in triumph.

Craig clapped. "Beer golf. It's a real thing."

John followed with a solid shot, then Stu, as ever, hit a precision laser, splitting the fairway. Craig smacked his, effortlessly smooth again, and watched it sail off past everyone else's.

"Show-off," Bruce muttered with a smile.

As the four walked off down the fairway, caddies trailing behind in the buggy's, the rest of the crew cheered and heckled, drinks in hand, ready for their turn — and the stories that would inevitably follow.

The sun was still blazing, the gamesmanship was heating up, and the golf — while occasionally brilliant — was clearly just the stage for the real theatre of the trip.

The back nine began with the same energy as a school trip after lunch — half buzzing, half barely functioning. Steve insisted on carrying his coconut for at least the next three holes.

"It's keeping me alive," he muttered, cradling it like a newborn. His swing was erratic, and at one point on the 12th, he accidentally teed off while still holding the straw in his mouth. The coconut stayed perched in the cup holder of the cart like some tropical mascot.

On the 13th, things got interesting. Danny, already struggling with the heat and nursing a dubious bunker count, hooked a low drive hard left into the jungle-fringed rough. Muttering under his breath, he wandered in with his caddie, machete-style, until he stopped dead. Right next to his ball, sunning itself lazily across the dusty undergrowth, was a slender green snake — flicking its tongue and eyeing up his Titleist like it had found breakfast. Danny turned slowly, eyes wide.

"Unplayable!" he shouted, leaping back. "New ball!"

His caddie took one look and nodded firmly. "Agreed."

"No penalty stroke," Danny yelled across to the others. "A bloody snake thinks my ball's its egg!"

Craig, watching from the fairway, cracked up.
"Lads, that's the most original drop rule I've ever heard."

Rory chimed in, "Next he'll be claiming a mongoose stole his putter."

Danny reappeared from the rough with a new ball, fanning himself and visibly rattled.

"I did not sign up for jungle golf."

Back on the 15th, Bruce attempted a heroic recovery shot from a clump of trees — the kind of shot that could either end up on the green or in the cart path. It went nowhere. Just a dull 'thud' and the ball dropped back at his feet.

"You see," he said without missing a beat, "I just wanted to make sure I had two attempts to enjoy this beautiful setting."

Eric was sweating like a chicken in a satay stall but managing to scramble pars and throwing in the occasional fist pump.

Bernard had gone oddly quiet, laser-focused, and racking up points without saying much — a man on a mission.

By the 17th, Stu and Craig were still neck and neck, both playing with almost irritating competence. Craig stuck his approach to six feet, Stu rolled in a curling birdie putt to keep the pressure on. The group reconvened again at the final tee — tired, sunburnt, and varying degrees of hydration.

Bruce leaned on his driver. "Whatever happens next, I want it known that I birdied the halfway beer hut and only lost two balls — one to water and one to wildlife."

Josh laughed. "Honestly, that snakes probably still confused why its egg dimples."

Steve looked down at his empty coconut in the back of the buggy. "I miss her already."

"Lads," Rory said, stretching his arms, "that was only round one. We've got three more days of this."

Danny looked up from his new, snake-free ball. "God help us."

They stepped off the 18th, not just as golfers — but as survivors. Back at the clubhouse, the group shuffled in, cheeks flushed and shirts sticking to backs from the heat and effort. The clinking of clubs against the racks echoed softly in the polished room as they dropped their gear and headed straight for the showers.

"Let's get ready to party, boys," Bruce called out, grinning. "Hurry up — the night won't wait for us!"

Steve groaned, peeling off his sunburned shirt. "If I don't get some aloe vera on this, I'll be glowing for days."

Bernard laughed as he shoved his bag onto a hook. "Come on, mate, you'll be glowing all night. Might help with the ladies."

Eric, still clutching a damp towel, glanced at his reflection. "Well, if this round was anything to go by, I'm lucky if I'm still standing by the end of the week."

"Don't worry," Stu said, pulling on a fresh shirt, "I hear the clubhouse food here's really good. We can all grab some grub before the real fun starts."

"Best kind of dinner," Craig added with a smirk, "food and a side of chaos." With that, refreshed and ready, they gathered up and headed down toward the restaurant, the buzz of the day giving way to the promise of an unforgettable evening.

Sitting at the table in the club's open-air restaurant, the group finally had a moment to relax. Bruce scanned the menu, nodding to himself. "Pad Kra Pao Gai for me," he said decisively.

Eric grinned. "I'll go for Pad Thai. Can't beat the classics." Steve, still nursing his bright-red sunburn, looked up and said, "Green curry for me."

Stu, ever the minimalist, shrugged. "Just some wings for me, thanks."
The others chimed in with their orders—Bernard went for the safer option, a burger and chips. Bruce raised an eyebrow and smirked. "Getting into the local cuisine then, Bernie?" he teased.

Bernard grinned, loosening the top buttons of his shirt again. "Hey, mate, I'm all for adventure, but some things you just can't fix — like a proper burger."

Bruce laughed, "Fair enough. Just wait till the street food later. You might change your mind, at least that'll loosen your pipes."

As the plates began to arrive, the chatter buzzed with anticipation for the rest of the week — the golf, the banter, and whatever else Phuket might throw at them.

Chapter Eight

Limbering Up for Round Two

The minibus came to a sharp stop as it pulled back into the resort driveway mid-afternoon, the golfers inside all wearing a combination of sunburn, weariness, and mild satisfaction. Clubs were left with the concierge, shoes kicked off, shirts unbuttoned.

Bruce stretched as he stepped off the last step of the bus, arching his back with a dramatic groan.

"That's me off for a massage," he announced. "Back's a bit sore after all that hero golf."

From a few rows back, Eric piped up with a grin, "Aye aye, we've heard that one before. Last time your back 'played up' you came back smelling of Tiger Balm and shame."

Unbothered, Bruce just winked. "Relaxation is key to performance, lads."

"I'll come with you," Bernard said, rubbing his lower back. "My old bones are twitching too." He paused. "And I've still got that blue pill in my wallet, just in case things get... therapeutic."

The others burst out laughing as the two wandered off toward the main street

"I'm heading to the pool," said John, stretching his arms over his head. "Need to cool off before the carnage resumes."

"Aye," Rory nodded. "We'll see you down there. Get the beers lined up."

One by one, the lads dispersed—some for rest, some for ice-cold Chang, and others for the mysterious world of Phuket massages. They all knew they had plenty of stories to write—and Bruce and Bernard were about to add a few more of their own. The two men stepped out from the cool confines of the resort and onto the bustling main street of Patong. The sun was dipping low, casting long shadows and igniting the neon signs beginning to flicker alive. Almost immediately, the air was filled with the chorus of voices.

"Hey sexy man! You want massage?" shouted a group of girls clustered outside a brightly lit shop. Bruce glanced at Bernard, who raised an eyebrow, a mixture of apprehension, anticipation and fear playing across his face. Together, they kept walking, feeling both the pull and the push—the lure of adventure and the nervous hesitation of two old friends out of their depth.

They passed dozens of shops with names like Heavenly Hands, Paradise Spa, and Tiger Touch. Each door seemed to promise the same sweet escape. The girls' calls came fast and thick, their smiles wide, voices enticing.

Then, just as they were about to turn a corner, the glowing sign Smooth and Relaxing caught their eye. The name was simple, promising exactly what they needed, plus the girls outside were beautiful.

Bruce looked at Bernard, who shrugged with a grin, "Well, why not?"

Before they fully registered what was happening, two stunning ladies appeared beside them, linking arms with each of the men and guiding them inside. The soft murmur of street noise faded away as they climbed a narrow staircase to private rooms upstairs.

The doors closed behind them, and the adventure really began. The rooms were dimly lit, soft Thai music playing in the background as Bernard and Bruce settled onto their massage mats laid out on the floor. The air was thick with the scent of essential oils and a faint hint of jasmine. The therapists began their work with practiced ease, kneading muscles and easing tension from long days of travel and golf.

Bruce sighed deeply as the knots in his back slowly loosened. Across in the next room, Bernard was trying to relax, but his eyes kept darting around, unsure what to expect.

As Bernard felt the therapist's hands glide over his shoulders and down his back, there came that faint and subtle hand glide across his buttocks. It was delicate enough to almost go unnoticed, but Bernard's instincts kicked in — he knew at that moment, the game was afoot.

He let out a small yelp, barely hiding his surprise, and glanced over at her. In the next room, Bruce was chuckling quietly to himself. The massage was definitely going to be an experience to remember. After about ninety minutes, Bruce and Bernard stepped out of the massage parlour into the warm Phuket evening, their faces lit with that unmistakable glow of pure satisfaction. Bruce slipped his shoes back on with a satisfied sigh, while Bernard adjusted his shirt collar, trying (and failing) to look casual.

"So, how was that then?" Bruce asked, eyes twinkling with curiosity.

Bernard grinned broadly, the kind of grin that said he'd been thoroughly pampered — and then some. "Bloody fantastic, me old fruit. Honestly, I can't get over how good it was. Eight quid for that? It's a steal. You don't get that kind of treatment back home."

Bruce laughed. "Yeah, but of course, I bet the 'happy ending' costs a bit more, right?"

Bernard chuckled. "Oh, without a doubt. But still, cheaper than a few beers, and a fish and chip supper in Leeds — and infinitely better for the back."

They both laughed, the sound easy and relaxed, the kind of laughter that only comes after a proper unwind. The tension from the week's travels and the morning's golf seemed to melt away with every step as they made their way back to the hotel.

As they approached the pool area, the familiar clinking of bottles and the murmur of their mates drifted toward them. The others were already gathered around the edge, sitting on lounge chairs, some with their feet dangling in the water, others just sprawled out, soaked in the sun, clutching bottles of Chang beer like it was the elixir of life.

"Ah, there you two are!" called out Eric, raising his bottle in greeting. "Thought you'd been kidnapped by the massage girls!"

Bruce shook his head with a grin. "Close enough. You wouldn't believe how good it was."

Bernard plopped down on the edge of the pool, the cool water lapping at his ankles. "I think I might have to come back for round two before the week's out."

"Yeah, yeah," teased Stu from his sun lounger. "Don't forget we've got a game tomorrow morning. You don't want to be too relaxed when we're teeing off."

"Relaxed and ready," Bernard shot back, winking. "You'll see."

The afternoon sun cast a golden glow across the water as the lads shared stories and laughed, the worries of travel and the stress of life back home slipping further away with every sip of beer and every easy smile. It was a moment to remember — a little slice of paradise in a week packed with golf, friendship, and just enough mischief to keep things interesting.

"Right, you drunken rabble, let's get up, I need a shit—shower, and a shave—and then hit Bangla for round two! Who's up for it?" Bruce said, getting out of his seat and not really waiting for an answer.

A massive cheer erupted around the poolside, laughter and cheers bouncing off the walls as the group began to break apart, the buzz of the afternoon slowly morphing into the electric anticipation of nightfall.

Steve caught Bernard as he was heading off and pulled him to one side, lowering his voice. "So, come on, spill it—what's the massage really like? Is it all as smooth as you made out? And, uh… can I come tomorrow if you guys go again?"

Bernard grinned knowingly, a glint in his eye.

"If we go, there's no question—you're definitely coming along. Time to pop your cherry, Steve." He chuckled and clapped him on the shoulder. They shared a knowing smile as they stepped into the lift together. The elevator doors slid shut, enclosing them in that brief, quiet pause between the chaotic afternoon and whatever madness the night would bring next.

Meanwhile, Bruce rounded up the others. "Seven thirty in the lobby. Don't be late!" he called out, already heading toward his room to freshen up.

The sun dipped low, painting the sky in fiery oranges and purples, as the men separated to prepare themselves. The promise of another night on Bangla Road hung heavy in the humid air—electric and impossible to ignore.

Within thirty minutes, they were all dressed and ready for action. Eric was grinning ear to ear—his luggage had finally arrived, so he was able to ditch the Thai boxing shorts for what he considered "sensible" clothes, though the rest of the group raised a few eyebrows at his questionable fashion choices.

"Right, boys," Bruce said, clapping his hands together, "a quick one here to kick off, then we'll start again proper at the Koala Bar. Tonight, we hit as many bars as possible on that strip—Bangla Road won't know what hit it."

Within twenty minutes, both Pete and Josh arrived, making their way through the bustling crowd toward the table.

"I picked Pete up on the way," Josh said with a smirk. "Had to get a full facial at the resort before coming out tonight— didn't want to scare anyone."

Bruce grinned and said loudly, "Bernard could've given you that treatment, Pete. He gave a girl named Jenny one earlier— slightly different, admittedly."

Laughter erupted around the table, and Steve, caught mid-sip, spat his beer out in surprise, earning a few amused glances and pats on the back. The night was warming up, and the boys were ready for whatever came next.

Laughter rippled through the group as they filed out of the hotel lobby, the warm night air buzzing with energy and the promise of chaos. The neon lights flickered in the distance, beckoning them into the wild heart of Phuket's nightlife.

Now back in the Koala Bar, the boys were soon deep in conversation with the girls and gathered around their table— flirty banter, laughter, and the occasional playful nudge filling the air. The neon lights of Bangla Road flickered and danced across their faces, adding to the buzz of the night. Just then, a street vendor sidled up to Eric, holding out a handful of watches, each one glinting under the street lamps.

"Sir, you want watch? Very good price, very nice watch," he said with a practiced grin. Eric shook his head with a chuckle, brushing his hand through his hair. "Haven't got time for a watch, mate," he replied with a smile. "I'm more interested in the time passing while I'm having fun."

The vendor laughed, undeterred, "Ah, time is money, my friend! But here, for you, special price—keep time and look good!"

Eric just shook his head again, raising his beer in a casual salute. "Thanks, but I'm better off losing track of time tonight."

The vendor muttered something in Thai and moved on, weaving through the crowd to find the next potential customer. Meanwhile, the boys carried on, caught between the charm of the night, the music, and the company of the locals who made Bangla Road come alive.

Right lads!" shouted Josh, grinning wide. "I fancy a go-go bar now — come on, my treat!"

The group veered off down a narrow side street, neon signs buzzing overhead, until they reached The Cheeky Girls — a notorious gogo bar tucked away behind an unassuming door. Josh pulled aside a thick velvet curtain, revealing the chaos inside.

The place was two stories of pure pandemonium. Up front, a stage stretched wide with pulsating lights and a crowd packed tight. Girls in glittering costumes danced and teased, while the smell of cheap beer and sweat mingled with the bass-heavy music vibrating through the floorboards. The lads found seats along the edge of the stage, grinning like kids in a candy shop. After fifteen minutes and two rounds of ice-cold beers, the anticipation in the room shifted. The lights dimmed further and suddenly the infamous ping pong show began.

Table tennis balls started flying everywhere — bouncing off heads, landing on tables, and occasionally ricocheting into drinks. One rogue ball careened through the air and plopped squarely into Danny's beer. He stared down at the floating sphere and turned to Keith with a grimace.

"I ain't touching that, mate — you don't know where that ball's been."

Keith just laughed and shook his head, pointing to a girl sprawled provocatively in the corner of the stage. "Don't be daft, lad. We know exactly where that ball came from."

Danny's eyes followed Keith's finger to the grinning lady, who winked and blew a kiss at the group.

The boys burst into laughter, the ridiculousness of the moment washing away any lingering hangovers or jet lag. The night was just getting started.

They continued drinking, girls sitting with them milking every baht they could out of them for lady drinks.

"Right lads, I'm off," slurred Bruce, swaying slightly as he drained the last of his beer. "Golf tomorrow morning at Pheonix Dunes. Bus leaves at ten sharp — don't say I didn't warn you."

Josh got the bill.

"What's the damage" Asked Rory.
"15,000 Baht replied Josh"
"kin ell, thanks for the treat" came the reply.
"My pleasure, can't take it with us!"

Eric looked up from his glass, his head wobbling under the weight of several Changs and a few questionable shots.

"That bugger Stu left hours ago," he muttered, eyes half-closed. "He's far too serious about this lark than we are."

Bernard leaned in, tapping Eric on the shoulder and whispering with a grin, "Maybe he just doesn't want to waste his money on wild women and beer... unlike us enlightened gentlemen."

The group erupted in laughter, swaying on their stools as the chaos of the go-go bar buzzed around them. Strobe lights flickered, music thumped, and a girl dressed as a nurse waved a feather boa in Bruce's direction as he stumbled toward the exit.

Rory suddenly stood tall — or as tall as his wobbling legs would allow — and raised both arms dramatically. "To bed, you horny toads!" he shouted with theatrical flair, drawing a few curious glances from the staff. And just like that, he led the half-cut parade out of The Cheeky Girls, a pied piper of battered men, staggering laughter, and the faint scent of tequila and regret — winding their way back through the neon-lit streets toward the sanctuary of their hotel.

Chapter Nine

The Pheonix Dunes Dash

The bus engine was already humming, the sun just starting to blaze, although there were some clouds in the Phuket sky. Nearly everyone was up and at it, a little fragile from the night before but buzzing for the next round at the stunning Pheonix Dunes. Clubs loaded, sunglasses on, and a round of groans as they clambered aboard.

"Right, where's Danny?" Bruce asked, looking down the list.

Back in his hotel room, Danny was still snoring like a bear in hibernation, tangled in a twisted white sheet with the faint glow of his phone screen lighting the bedside table. He had optimistically set his alarm for 9:30. But when it buzzed, he lazily swiped snooze with the grace of a man who hadn't quite made peace with the morning.

Back on the bus, Eric looked at his watch. "It's five past ten. What shall we do, lads?"

"Leave the lazy sod!" he added with a grin, earning a round of chuckles.

"Let's hit the fairways," Bruce said, slamming the door shut behind him. With that, the engine roared, and the bus rolled out of the hotel car park, leaving one man behind.

At 10:05, Danny sat bolt upright, blinking at the clock in disbelief. "Shit." He scrambled around the room, throwing on clothes in a frenzy, tripping over a sandal, and jabbing out a message to Bruce:

"I'll see you at the club. Did you take my clubs?"

Bruce's reply came back almost instantly:
"No bro. They're in storage where you left them."

"Shit again." Now in full panic mode, Danny bolted down to the storage area, located his clubs (thankfully untouched), and ran to the street. There, he flagged down the first motorbike taxi he saw. "Pheonix Dunes Golf Club — now, now, now!" he shouted, slinging the bag across his back like a soldier off to war. The bemused driver just nodded, popped a helmet on

Danny's head, and off they went. Moments later, up ahead on the winding road, the bus appeared. Danny's eyes lit up.

"Catch them!" he yelled over the wind. As the bike pulled up alongside the bus, Danny waved frantically with one hand, trying not to fall off. Inside the bus, Eric glanced out the window, squinting through his sunglasses. "Would you look at that…" Then, with a perfectly timed gesture, Eric slowly raised his middle finger toward the glass.

Everyone on the bus burst out laughing, banging the windows and shouting out half-sober taunts as the bus driver — perhaps encouraged — pressed a little harder on the accelerator. Danny watched helplessly as the bus sped off, leaving him in a trail of diesel and mockery. "Straight to the club, mate," Danny said, slumping against the driver's back.

And so, with clubs bouncing on his back and adrenaline pumping through his body, Danny zoomed through the Thai countryside like some mad outlaw golfer chasing his crew — determined not to miss a single swing. Halfway to the club, with the jungle thick on either side and the road snaking like a lazy python through the hills, the heavens opened with tropical fury. One minute, the sun was blazing. The next, it was like God had tipped a bucket over the island.

Danny looked up just in time for a face full of monsoon rain. "Are you fkin kidding me?!" Within seconds, he was soaked to the skin, his T-shirt clinging to him like clingfilm, his golf bag turning into a waterlogged sponge. The motorbike weaved through the puddles like a surfboard in a storm, its driver unfazed as if this was just another Tuesday.

By the time they pulled into the Pheonix Dunes Golf Club car park, Danny looked like a drenched rat who'd barely survived a shipwreck. Steam rose from the heat of the tarmac and the sudden coolness of the rain. The tour bus had arrived just minutes earlier, and as Danny dismounted — sodden, hair plastered to his head, shoes squelching — a round of raucous cheers erupted from the boys waiting under the club's canopy.

"Danny-boy! Look what the storm dragged in!" shouted Keith.

"You look like a soggy caddie," laughed Bernard.

"Proper drowned hamster," added Eric.

Danny stood there dripping, flipping the bird with both hands as his bag slipped sideways on his shoulder.

Bruce clapped him on the back — a wet slap of palm on soaked shirt. "Well done for showing up, mate. That deserves a beer."

He turned to the group. "Right lads, beer time while this rain clears up. Let's not get our knickers in a twist about tee times." They all made their way toward the clubhouse terrace, where cold beers, covered seating, and dry towels awaited.

Danny flopped into a chair, water still dripping off his cap. "I need a pint and a towel... in that order," he muttered.

"Don't worry," said Bruce, handing him a Chang, "we'll all be swinging soon enough... and not the kind you lot were into last night."

Laughter broke out again as thunder cracked in the distance — another wild chapter of their Thai adventure still unfolding. The rain finally gave up its tantrum just as the group drained the last of their terrace beers. The clouds still loomed, sulky and grey, but the fairways of The Pheonix Dunes glistened with a post-storm sheen, steam rising gently off the drenched grass. The boys, in high spirits and a dazzling array of golf attire — Bernard in neon green shorts and a flamingo-print polo, Keith wearing a hat shaped like a pineapple, and Eric looking like a Hawaiian bar tender — made their way to the first tee.

Steve's caddie walked towards him holding two vey muddy golf balls she had pulled from his bag. Her head on a slant, and with a wry smile she asked, "Would you like me to wash your balls Mr. Steve?" Steve spat out his beer and looked mouth wide open.

"That's the best offer you'll get mate, but she means your golf balls, so settle down". Shouted Keith! All the caddies burst into laughter. Danny still looked like a drowned rat, water squelching from his shoes with each step, his hair stuck flat to his forehead. He pulled his cap down low in a feeble attempt to hide the fact he resembled something rescued from a canal.

Bruce stepped confidently onto the tee, his caddie Chat — yet another Thai stunner in a beautiful caddie outfit, clung to her body as if it had been tailored, and a cheeky grin — handing him the driver with flair.

"Right, my darling," Bruce said with a wink, gripping the club. "Time to show these degenerates what the Brewster can do." He teed it up with exaggerated ceremony, adjusted his glove, gave the lads a theatrical bow, then smashed the ball 260 yards dead straight down the middle.

A moment of silence followed. Then roaring applause and jeering from the boys.

"Clear evidence," Bruce said smugly, shouldering his driver like a rifle, "that Chang beer improves my swing. Might bottle it and sell it as performance fuel." The rest of the front nine was a mix of brilliance, banter, and pure chaos. On the third hole, Danny — still wet and grumpy — took a mighty swing on a downhill par 4, slipped on the slick grass, and ended up sliding twenty feet down the hill on his backside, mud streaked from his shoulders to his socks.

"Oh great," he muttered, "I've invented Thailand's first human luge."

"Nice form!" shouted Pete, barely able to hold his phone steady while filming it.

Keith wasn't much better. On the fifth, he tried to recover a ball from the edge of the rough, misjudged the slope, and tumbled headfirst into a bush. Only his pineapple hat was visible as the group howled with laughter.

"Keith, mate, we told you to find the green — not become it!" Bernard yelled as they dragged him out, covered in leaves and beetles.

Steve, ever the quiet assassin, played surprisingly well. Every time someone took the piss out of him, he just quietly sank a long putt and walked off whistling. By the seventh hole, they were starting to suspect he was actually some kind of golfing monk.

Eric, meanwhile, claimed every bad shot was down to "club sabotage" and insisted his caddie was holding the clubs at the wrong angle. When asked if perhaps the problem lay in the user, he told them all to "shove it where the monsoon don't reach."

By the time they hit the ninth, everyone was muddy, sweaty, and in various stages of sunburn or hangover recovery. But the laughter hadn't stopped. Bruce cracked open another beer from his golf bag cooler and held it aloft.

"Lads," he announced. "Golf may be a gentleman's game — but we are certainly not gentlemen."

They clinked cans and bottles, the echoes of their laughter rolling across the soaked fairways of Pheonix Dunes.

Bruce stood at the tee of the picturesque par-3, a glint in his eye and a wad of notes in hand. "Right, lads! Time for the 500-baht caddie challenge," he announced, raising his voice just enough for the caddies to gather around. "Here's how it works—nearest the pin wins the whole pot. Winner takes all."

He turned to the assembled group of bright-eyed Thai caddies. "Okay, you gorgeous bunch, listen up. Each of us has put in 500 baht, and the closest to the pin on this hole takes the lot. It's a tidy little sum for one lucky lady—so give it your best!"

A ripple of giggles and excitement ran through the caddies as they eyed the pin sitting about 135 yards out, surrounded by a moat of sand traps and a small pond for good measure. The lads stepped back, smirking, expecting a bit of light-hearted competition. But what followed was anything but casual.

One by one, the caddies stepped up with elegant, relaxed swings—and promptly started landing shots on the green with surgeon-like precision. The lads stood slack jawed as the balls began peppering the putting surface like pro tour highlights.

Keith turned to Pete. "Are we sure they're not ex-LPGA or something? I can't even get my ball airborne most days!"

Bruce watched in stunned admiration as Chat, his own caddie and the undisputed crowd favourite, stepped up with a grin and no practice swing. She launched her shot high into the air with a smooth rhythm and graceful follow-through. The ball pitched once, checked up, and stopped three feet from the hole. The group erupted in applause.

"Well," Bruce said, raising an eyebrow and cracking open another beer from his bag, "I'd say that deserves a cold one. To Chat—queen of the fairway and newly crowned champion of the 500-baht challenge!" They all laughed and handed over the winnings as Chat gave a little bow and blew them a kiss. The caddies high-fived, clearly enjoying their well-earned bragging rights, while the lads shook their heads in mock disbelief.

Danny muttered, "Remind me next time not to challenge women who carry clubs for a living..."

Eric raised his beer, "To being humbled—in style!"
And with that, they strolled to the green, their egos slightly bruised, but their spirits sky high.

With spirits still sky high after the 500-baht caddie challenge and a day of laughable, mud-splattered golf, the lads wrapped up their final putts on the 18th and made their way back toward the clubhouse. A few playfully argued over who'd "won," though it was clear none of them remembered their actual scores.

Inside the changing rooms, the air was thick with steam and banter. "I swear half my round was played in a bunker," said Danny, towelling off.
"At least you found them. I was too busy rolling down hills like a bloody toddler," laughed Pete.

Keith held up his muddy shorts. "These need to be burned, not washed."

Freshly showered and changed, they settled into the open-air bar that overlooked the course. The breeze was warm, the beer was cold, and the scent of grilled meat drifted from the kitchen.

"Right, what's everyone having?" Bruce asked, squinting at the menu. "I'm starving."

"Pad Thai for me," said Eric. "Keep it local."

"Burger and chips," said Keith. "After today, I need comfort food."

"I want something with spice," said Bernard. "Set fire to my taste buds and see if I can still feel anything after that round."

"You sure about that?" Pete chimed in. "Last time you had something spicy you were sweating like a certain Prince in a Pizza Express."

Laughter exploded around the table. As the food arrived, plates clattering and bottles being refilled, Bruce leaned in with that familiar twinkle in his eye.

"Right lads, listen up. Tomorrow we've got no golf, no plans. So, I say we make the most of it. I've sorted us a boat trip— to James Bond Island, and a few other spots. Not the touristy crap, mind you—just us. Private boat. Bit of exploring. Bit of beach. Bit of banter. All in, it's £180 each. You in?"

Nods and mumbles of agreement followed, as mouths were too full to speak clearly.

"And," Bruce continued with a knowing smirk, "I say we spice it up. Let's not just have a boat full of sweaty old blokes. I say we invite some chicks to join us. Liven the trip up a bit."

Bernie raised his beer. "Too bloody right, old lad! We can't be surrounded by your wrinkly mugs all day."

Danny chuckled. "Just make sure they're not as good at swimming as those caddies were at golf—don't think my ego can handle another hit."

The plan was sealed with a round of beers, the kind of moment where the day fades into night with laughter, full stomachs, and the promise of even more mischief tomorrow.

"First though boys, we need to go fishing tonight. Each man has to pull a chick for the boat trip, even you Steve!"

They all laughed as Steve turned a shade of red.

"Back to the hotel!"

As they strolled into the hotel lobby, weary but content after a long day of golf, Bruce's sharp eyes caught something the others missed—a large white sign propped on an easel by reception. In bold letters, it read:

"Welcome to Songkran! Tomorrow marks the start of Thailand's New Year water festival. Please be aware that you may be sprayed with water in the streets as part of the celebrations."

Bruce froze mid-step, eyes lighting up with mischief.

"Oh, no, no, no," he muttered with a wicked grin. "Can't have the lads knowing this…"

While the rest of the group ambled ahead toward the lifts, deep in conversation about boat trips and beachwear, Bruce casually sauntered over to the sign. Looking around to make sure no staff were watching; he grabbed the edge of the placard and dragged it behind a giant potted plant—one of those big artificial things with shiny green leaves and a ceramic base.

He stepped back, checked it was fully obscured, then nodded to himself in satisfaction.

"Right," he chuckled under his breath. "We can't have those lot being forewarned, can we? Let the games begin. This... is going to be brilliant."

Whistling innocently, he turned and joined the others at the lift, hands in his pockets, already imagining the chaos that awaited that evening.

Chapter Ten

Operation Scouting for Boat Babes

By 7:30 p.m., the boys had all gathered in the hotel bar, showered, ironed, and topped up with aftershave like it was a magic elixir. Shirts ranged from loud florals to even louder neon—each of them ready to hit the town. Spirits were high, and beers were already flowing.

Josh and Pete had agreed to meet them at Koala Bar, their usual stomping ground. What they didn't know, thanks to a cheeky heads-up from Bruce, was that the boys had a secret: the Songkran water festival officially kicked off the next morning. But Bruce had made it very clear over the phone.

"Listen mate," Bruce said, stifling a laugh, "say nothing about Songkran to the others. I've already hidden the hotel sign. This is going to be comedy gold when the water starts flying. Let's keep them dry and clueless."

"You're evil," Pete had replied, chuckling. "I love it."

Now, reunited at Koala Bar, the group took their usual corner near the front where the fans spun lazily overhead, and the Chang was served ice-cold. The same girls from the night before welcomed them with big smiles and cries of "Welcome back, boys!"

Drinks were ordered without a word. Bruce, never one to waste time, raised his bottle.

"Right, gentlemen," he said, glancing around the group like a football manager giving a pep talk. "Tomorrow, the boat trip to James Bond Island is happening. Our own boat. No tourists. Just us, some beers, and—hopefully—a few lovely ladies to keep things interesting."

"Amen to that!" Rory said, raising his glass.

"So tonight," Bruce continued, "we're on a scouting mission. Let's find a few charming companions to invite aboard. Keep it respectful, but aim high, lads. If we're sailing, let's sail in style."

Bernie grinned, already a few sips ahead. "I'll have 'em queuing up, Brucey. Just point me in the right direction."

"I bet you will, you old fox," Eric laughed. "I'll settle for one with teeth this time."

The whole table erupted. With drinks downed and egos inflated, the boys stood up and began their slow march down Bangla Road. Music thundered from every open door, lights flickered in neon madness, and the streets were thick with tourists, dancers, hustlers, and the odd fire-juggler. Their mission was simple: chat, charm, and recruit a few friendly faces for tomorrow's cruise. As they passed one bar, a group of girls waved from a balcony. Steve pointed up.

"Reckon they'll want a boat trip?"

"No idea," Danny replied, "but I bet they'll want a few drinks first."

Bruce smiled as he surveyed the chaos, imagining the drenched mayhem that awaited them all in the morning. But tonight was about scouting—and the first round of madness was just getting started.

Eric was the first to make his move. Back at Koala Bar, he'd taken a shine to one of the girls working behind the bar—a cheeky, petite brunette called Fon who had a laugh louder than the stereo and eyes that sparkled with mischief. As they were about to move on, Eric leaned over to her and said,

"We're heading out, love, but I reckon you should come on this boat trip tomorrow. I need someone to make sure I don't fall in."

Fon grinned, flicked her hair, and replied, "Only if you promise to wear those sexy swim shorts again, and pay me 3000 baht."

"Deal," Eric beamed, give me your line number and I'll message you later when and where to meet tomorrow"

And just like that, Eric had locked in his plus 1. The boys strolled down Bangla Road, moving from bar to bar like moths to neon. In each place, they turned on the charm with varying degrees of success. Danny was soon deep in conversation with a tall, leggy woman named Tip, who seemed to find his awkward Northern banter irresistible. Rory paired off with a girl called Nok who, despite barely understanding a word he said, found him hilarious and had a laugh that made his heart skip. Bernie, somehow, had managed to attract two—though whether they were genuinely interested or just loved his terrible dance moves was anyone's guess. More than likely the thickness of his wallet was the attraction.

Only Steve remained unpartnered.

He nursed a beer quietly at the edge of one bar while the rest of the lads were getting numbers and making plans. Bruce noticed. He nudged Pete. "Poor bugger's struggling tonight. Bit like a fish in a tree, our Steve."

Pete laughed, finishing the rest of his bottle. "Got an idea?" Bruce's eyes glinted. "Come on. I know a place. Bit... different. But trust me. Right lads, follow me"

The two lead the way and headed down a narrow side alley lit by a single flickering red bulb. At the end was a smaller, tucked-away bar called Velvet Dreams, pulsing with music and mystery. Bruce opened the door with a grin. Inside, the place was glamorous, sultry, and packed with ladyboys—some so stunning you'd swear they'd just stepped out of a magazine shoot. Steve was last to follow them in, unsuspecting, before stopping dead in his tracks.

"Bloody hell… are you sure this isn't a fashion show, these ladies are gorgeous?"

Bruce clapped him on the back. "Look lively, mate. You might meet someone who actually laughs at your jokes."

Just then, a vision in a tight red dress appeared before them. Tall, with flawless skin, legs that went on for days, and a dazzling smile—she introduced herself as Peemai Sukme.

Steve blinked. "Sorry, your name's… what?"

"Peemai," she replied, "but my friends call me 'Suki'." She said winking back at him.

Bruce stifled a laugh and whispered to Pete, "He's gone. Look at his face. Love at first sight."

Steve, red-faced and already half-smitten, spent the rest of the evening talking to Suki, completely enchanted. She laughed at his jokes, teased him gently, and called him "Stevie Baby," which only made the others roar.

"Bruce, I think I'm in love with her" Said Steve, staring at Suki.

"Good for you mate, but you might be getting a little more in your package than you thought" said Bruce laughing.

Steve took Suki's line number and had already arranged to meet her for breakfast at the hotel before going on the boat trip.

"Not taking her back then Steve?" asked Eric.

"No, she's perfect. I'm taking my time"

By the time they regrouped, most of the boys had girls in tow and stories already forming. As they stumbled back toward the hotel, Bruce looked around at the motley crew.

"Right lads," he said with a grin. "Tomorrow, we sail—with possibly the most colourful passenger list in Phuket."

Bernie threw an arm around Tip and slurred, "We're gonna need a bigger boat."

Laughter filled the street, and the night echoed with mischief. What none of them knew was that by sunrise, the city would be soaked—and so would their plans.

"Right lads let's get some kip. See you all down in the foyer at 9:00 a.m." With that, they all trotted off to their rooms.

The next morning, everyone was down promptly. Steve had messaged Suki and was waiting for her in the street outside. Barely five minutes later, he stormed back into the foyer— Suki chasing after him—both of them drenched from head to toe.

Water dripped from Steve's hair. His linen shirt clung to his chest like a soggy tea towel, and his once-stylish loafers squelched with every furious step.

"Some f*in' idiot just launched a bucket of water at me the second I stepped outside!" he shouted, eyes wide with disbelief. "Then some clown on a scooter blasted me with a bloody super soaker! What the hell is going on out there?"

The lads burst into laughter, nearly spilling their coffees. Bruce tried to keep a straight face but failed miserably. "Ah, yeah... forgot to mention—it's Songkran today. Thai New Year. Water everywhere. It's how they celebrate."

"You forgot to mention?" Steve flapped his arms like an angry, soaked bird. "I look like I crawled out of a canal! My best shirt! My lucky pants! I bought those in Marbella!"

"Make sure Suki knows I've gone up to change," he added, stomping toward the lift. "Tell her it's not my fault. This is a bloody disaster!"

Keith called after him, grinning: "Might want to pack a poncho next time, Casanova!"

"Or a snorkel," Danny added.

As the lift doors closed on a soggy, fuming Steve, the rest of the lads collapsed into another round of laughter. Bruce leaned in, smirking: "Best boat trip ever—and we haven't even left the lobby."

Chapter Eleven

The Man with the Golden Boat

"All aboard!" Bruce called out as the last of the crew climbed onto the minibus waiting outside the hotel. Every seat was taken—lads in their shades and beach shirts, ladies in strappy dresses and oversized sunglasses, each holding iced coffees, bottles of water, or mystery cocktails in plastic cups. There was an electric buzz in the air.

Bruce stood at the front, doing a quick headcount. "All the ladies present?" he asked with a grin, then added with a smirk, "...and a few who aren't quite sure yet?" That got a roar of laughter from the back of the bus, with Steve going red and trying not to smile as Suki batted her lashes at him. With a nod, Bruce clapped his hands. "Right then, to the marina!"

As the bus rumbled off down the coast road, music played low in the background, and a couple of beers popped open despite the hour. Bernie, of course, had started on a rum and Coke at 9:20 AM.

When they arrived at the marina, the boat was waiting—sleek, white, and far too fast-looking for a group this hungover. As everyone stepped aboard, Bruce made a grand entrance, climbing aboard last with a flourish. He was wearing a battered old pirate hat, a black eye patch over one eye, and a water pistol tucked into his belt.

"Right, my landlubbers!" he shouted, arms wide like a man born for this role. "Today, we cruise like kings! James Bond-style, baby—but with cheaper beer, a Bond girl each, and more suncream!"

Laughter erupted across the deck as the engine kicked in and the boat eased away from the dock, headed out into the sparkling Andaman Sea.

As a tourist boat came alongside them, Eric shouted "Geez, look how those poor buggers are packed in there, like sardines!"

Josh raised his drink. "To the Bond boat and the beauties aboard!"

"To sun, sea, and slightly suspect decisions!" added Eric.

And with that, they sailed off into a day they'd be talking about for years.

The boat sliced through the sparkling waters, the warm sun beating down and a gentle breeze keeping spirits high. As the silhouette of James Bond Island came into view, the group gathered at the bow, snapping photos and teasing each other about who would be the first to jump in.

Bruce, still rocking his pirate hat and eye patch, swaggered over to the helm. "Alright crew, we've got a full day of exploring ahead. Swim, snorkel, maybe a little sunbathing, and definitely some embarrassing photos for later."

Once moored, the group scrambled off the boat and onto the famous limestone karsts. The narrow pathways were crowded with tourists, but Bruce had insisted on a less touristy side cove for a quieter swim.

As they trekked, Bernie slipped on a wet rock and fell flat on his backside, sending mud flying onto Josh's pristine white shorts.

"Welcome to the jungle, mate!" Josh shouted, laughing as he wiped the mud from his leg.

Bernie grinned, "At least I'm the only one adding some natural decoration around here."

"Right lads let's have a photo in front of this rock," Bruce called out, already lining up the shot on his phone.

As the group shuffled into position, Danny shouted, "Steve—you can be Nick Nack!"

Laughter burst out as Steve struck a pose, crouching slightly with a mock-menacing grin.

"Alright, now one with the ladies," Bruce said, waving everyone together. "That's the one for the wives."

He snapped a few more, then added with a smirk, "And now one for your private collection, you bunch of perverts!" With the pictures taken and everyone in high spirits, they pulled anchor and motored toward a sheltered bay.

Soon, bodies were flying off the boat and into the water—laughing, splashing, racing across the surface like kids on holiday. Bernie, still nursing sore ribs from the earlier mud incident, attempted a grand dive... only to bellyflop with a thunderous smack. A wave of cheers and howls followed as he surfaced, coughing and grinning.

"Graceful as ever, mate!" someone shouted.

Not everyone jumped in. At the edge of the deck, Suki stood barefoot, eyeing the water. "I can't swim," she said to Steve, her deep voice casual, but clipped. Steve glanced down at her, raising an eyebrow. Her words sounded simple enough—but there was something unreadable in her tone. A flicker of discomfort. Was she just nervous, or was she hiding something... something that lurked not in the water, but perhaps beneath the fabric of her bikini bottoms? Steve gave a half-smile and turned toward the others.

"We'll stay on the boat," he announced. "Didn't fancy a swim anyway."

And with that, they settled in on the sun-warmed deck—just the two of them, watching from above as the others splashed and laughed below. Beers in hand, sunglasses on, and something unspoken hovering quietly between them. After an hour of swimming, the group clambered back on board. Sun-kissed and waterlogged, they sprawled across the deck with cold beers in hand, passing around crisps and swapping stories as the sun dipped lower in the sky. The kind of day that sticks to your memory like salt on your skin. The boat slowed as it neared the jagged limestone cliffs, where a dark opening marked the entrance to the caves. The captain handed out hard hats with a knowing grin.

"Mind your heads in there. Some of it's quite low," he said. One by one, they disembarked onto the rocks. Some of the group settled near the entrance, happy to sit, chat, and take photos. The moment they stepped inside, the temperature dropped noticeably—the air inside the cave was much cooler than the warmth outside, offering a welcome break from the sun.

Steve and Suki lingered at the back before slipping away from the group and venturing deeper into the cave, their hard hats casting beams of light across the damp stone walls. Stalactites and stalagmites surrounded them, creating a natural cathedral of stone.

As they moved further in, the chatter from the entrance faded behind them. Shadows flickered across the rock face, and the air grew still and cool. Suddenly, Suki stopped, turned, and looked at Steve with a sly smile. Without warning, she stepped close, placed a hand gently on his chest, and lowered herself to her knees.

"Relax," she said softly. "Just go with it."

Moments later, a loud, involuntary yelp burst from Steve's throat. The sharp echo bounced through the cave system, growing louder as it travelled all the way back to the entrance. Bruce paused mid-conversation, then looked over at Bernie, grinning.

"I reckon that was little Steve's cherry bursting."

Bernie raised an eyebrow, cracking a smirk.
"Maybe. Whatever it was—something definitely happened to him that's never happened before."

The lads laughed, shrugged it off, and passed around another beer. Deeper in the cave, Steve was catching his breath—and grinning like a man who'd just discovered something life-changing. A little while later, Suki and Steve emerged from the shadows of the cave, walking hand in hand. Steve looked flushed, dazed almost—like he'd just come out of a sauna and won the lottery at the same time. Suki, ever composed, calmly dabbed at her dress with a wet wipe, not quite hiding the smirk on her face. As the pair stepped into view, the lads fell silent for half a second—then Rory threw his arms in the air.

"Oggi, Oggi, Oggi!" he shouted.

"Oi! Oi! Oi!" the others roared back in unison, their voices echoing off the cave walls.

Laughter erupted as they surrounded Steve, clapping him on the back. Bernie grinned and stepped forward.

"Welcome to the club, young man," he said. "About bloody time!" Steve tried to act casual, but his grin gave him away. Suki leaned against the rock nearby, arms folded, watching it all with an arched brow and quiet satisfaction.

The captain, standing by the boat with a bemused look, gave a slight nod that said he'd seen this sort of thing before. He waved a hand toward the deck.

"Right, everyone aboard. Sun's not going to wait for you lot. We are finishing off at the secluded beach where you can have two hours."

They clambered back on board, still chuckling. The engine rumbled to life, the boat turning gently back toward open water, the water so clear you could see schools of fish beneath. As the cliffs faded behind them, the group sprawled across the deck—sun-kissed, half-salted, and a little more bonded than before. And Steve, hand still loosely laced with Suki's, leaned back with a satisfied sigh. Yeah... something had definitely changed.

Within twenty minutes, they arrived at the secluded beach, a hidden gem framed by lush jungle and crystal-clear water. Without hesitation, everyone jumped off the boat and waded toward the shore. Bruce and Rory lugged the large cool boxes, half-filled with beers, their arms straining but spirits high.

Once on land, the group paired off with their ladies and slowly dispersed into the thick greenery, exploring the jungle's secrets—and maybe taking a few detours of their own to investigate some personal mysteries.

Steve and Suki stayed behind, settling comfortably on a towel, under a large parasol the captain had provided. Stu joined them, launching into a detailed rundown of his game plan for the golf course the next day. Steve, already relaxed, gave a lazy thumb-up.

"Carry on, Stu. This talk's going to send me straight to sleep for an hour."

Stu grinned, undeterred, and continued plotting his perfect swing while Steve closed his eyes, letting the gentle sounds of the beach and jungle wash over him.

After a while, the soothing coolness of the water was too tempting to resist. Steve and Suki waded in, joining the others as they slipped beneath the surface. Laughter echoed as they raced and splashed, the turquoise sea sparkling under the sun. Bruce and Rory took it easy, floating nearby while keeping an eye on the cool boxes and making sure the beers stayed cold. The group savoured the moment — carefree and refreshed. As the afternoon sun began to dip, casting golden hues across the water, the captain called out from the boat.

"Alright, folks! Time to head back!"

Reluctantly, they swam toward the shore, their limbs heavy but spirits high. Back on the sand, they gathered their things, towels and bags, and prepared to board the boat once again. Steve shook the water from his hair and smiled at Suki.

"Ready to head back?"

She nodded, slipping her hand into his as they joined the others, their laughter mingling with the gentle crash of the waves.

Once back on land, they boarded the bus and headed back to the hotel. The ladies all waved goodbye and said they hoped to see them later. Steve lingered with Suki, he had already arranged to meet her back in the foyer at 8:00pm. With that, the boys headed to their rooms.

"Right lads" said Bruce, I'm off for a kip then we can head out into the madness of Songkran, don't put your best gear on tonight! Meet in the bar at 7:45"

Chapter Twelve

Out of Bounds, and Out of Sight

Sandra was looking out of her front bedroom window, enjoying the slow start to the day. From up there she could see half the street — the postman weaving from gate to gate, Mrs. Hall from number 7 fussing over her roses, and a stray crisp packet drifting lazily in the breeze. It was the kind of morning that felt... uneventful. Then she spotted Bev. It was like watching a weather front roll in — all energy and dark clouds. Bev was in full march, arms swinging with military precision, handbag clamped tight, jaw set like she was heading into a disciplinary meeting she had called herself. The poor dog at the end of the lead was trotting desperately behind her, little legs going double speed just to keep up. Sandra frowned in amusement. "Oh dear... that's a 'tell you everything' march if I've ever seen one," she murmured to herself.

By the time Bev reached the driveway, her hair had escaped its clip, and her sunglasses — which she was still wearing despite the cloudy sky — had slid halfway down her nose. The dog's lead was wrapped around her wrist twice over, probably for grip in case the poor creature decided enough was enough and made a dash for freedom. The knock on Sandra's door wasn't so much a knock, as an attempted demolition. Four sharp bangs, a pause, then another three, just to make sure the message was clear: I am here, I am angry, and you will let me in. Sandra opened the door with the same unhurried calm she'd had upstairs, leaning casually against the frame. She took in the scene — Bev's flustered face, windswept hair, the slightly wild look in her eyes — and gave her a deliberately neutral greeting.

"Hi, Bev. How's things?" she asked, eyebrow raising in quiet curiosity. Bev's reply was instant and explosive.

"How's bloody things, how's bloody things? How d'you think? Can I come in or do I need to knock the door down?"

Sandra stepped back, gesturing her inside like a maître d' welcoming a VIP.

"Come in, come in. What's the emergency?"

The dog skittered across the hallway tiles like a curling stone, immediately finding a corner to sniff. In the kitchen, Sandra nodded towards the counter.

"Coffee? Tea? Or… something stronger?"

Bev's eyes lit up, the way someone's do when they've just spotted the dessert trolley. "Got anything stronger? Please say yes."

Sandra chuckled, glancing at the clock. "It's only half nine in the morning, you know." She said it like she was about to refuse… then, without missing a beat, reached into the cupboard and pulled out a bottle of red wine.

Bev's expression softened instantly.

"God bless you, Sandra."

Pouring a generous glass — and making a mental note that "just a splash" was not in Bev's vocabulary — Sandra slid it across the table.

"Aren't you having one?" Bev asked hopefully. Sandra shook her head.

"No, no. A bit early for me. I'll stick to tea. One of us needs to remember what's said today."

Bev took a deep breath, downed half the glass in one go, then swirled the rest as though the motion alone might calm her down.

"Right. I woke up Saturday morning, and Eric… he'd gone. Gone with the wind. And not just him — his golf clubs." Sandra's eyes narrowed slightly.

"Gone? What do you mean, gone?"

"The whole bloody lot," Bev said, hand raking through her hair. "The bag, the clubs, and my best bloody suitcase! — vanished into thin air. No note, no text, not a word. Just… disappeared."
Sandra pulled out a chair and sat opposite her.

"Have you called him? Texted him?"

"Of course," Bev snapped. "No answer. Left a voicemail. Nothing." Her voice cracked slightly, a mix of fury and the faintest touch of hurt.

Sandra took a slow sip of tea.

"Do you have any idea where he might be? Anywhere he'd go without telling you?"

Bev shook her head. "No clue. I thought maybe the golf club, or a mate's place, but nothing. It's like he's vanished off the face of the earth."

Sandra gave a small, knowing smile. "Actually… I think I know where he is."

Bev leaned forward so fast the wine in her glass sloshed dangerously. "You do?"

Sandra nodded, lowering her voice like she was revealing state secrets. "Thailand. All of them — the clubs and Eric — are in Thailand."

Bev blinked. "Thailand? What on earth would Eric be doing going all the way out there?"

Sandra shrugged. "Who knows? Maybe a last-minute holiday, or some crazy golf tournament I don't know about. But I'm sure he's there with John and Bruce."

Bev let out a laugh that was more bark than chuckle. "A last-minute holiday? He didn't even say goodbye. Not a word."

Sandra reached out and patted her hand. "Sometimes people need to get away, but this has been planned for months, I'm surprised you didn't know. Maybe this is his way of finding a little peace — or trouble."

Bev took another gulp of wine. "I'll give him bloody peace when he gets back. I'll knock his bleeding block off when I see him, assuming he ever comes back!"

Sandra smiled gently. "Well, one thing's for sure: he's in Thailand. I heard John and Bruce talking about who was going, so I'm sure he's safe. He's a good guy, Eric!"

Bev frowned. "Aren't you bothered they've all gone to Thailand?"

"Nope. I hope they're having a fabulous time. Remember, Bev — our husbands are actually decent blokes, so letting them have a bit of fun is not a lot to ask."

Bev sighed. "True, Eric is a decent guy. I just wish he'd told me. I'm just so disappointed he didn't."

Sandra shrugged. "He maybe knew you would have reacted as you have. Time to be nice to each other. Life is too short to argue all the time!"

"Tell you what, Bev — I'll send John a text and ask Eric to get in touch, so at least you know he's safe."

"Thanks, Sandra. That would be a big help. Any chance of a refill?"

Sandra topped up her glass, thinking back to the last time Eric had "vanished." It had been three years ago, after the infamous barbecue incident. He'd told Bev he was going to "nip to B&Q for lighter fluid" and somehow ended up in Wales at a fishing lodge with his mates for an entire weekend. The only reason Bev had found out was because he'd accidentally posted a selfie on Facebook holding a trout. Sandra smirked at the memory.

"At least this time he took the golf clubs instead of a fishing rod," she muttered.

Bev gave her a suspicious look. "What was that?"

"Nothing," Sandra said, sipping her tea, though her eyes still glinted with amusement.

The two women sat quietly for a moment, the dog finally curling up at Bev's feet, its breathing slowing now that it had survived the morning's march. Outside, the postman's whistle drifted faintly through the open window, a strangely peaceful soundtrack to Bev's domestic storm.

Back at the hotel, Bruce was rudely awakened by the shrill buzz of his alarm. He groaned, rolled over, then dragged himself to the bathroom. One look in the mirror made him wince.

"Jesus," he muttered. "I look like a bloody tomato." His face was a perfect shade of crimson, a painful reminder of too much sun and not enough sunscreen.

Meanwhile, in the next room, Bernie hadn't even managed to get undressed before passing. He stirred groggily on top of the covers, still fully clothed and looking like he'd been dragged backwards through a sand dune.

"My bloody head," he groaned, shuffling toward the bathroom like a zombie. "I'm definitely too old for this shite."

Back in John's room his phone buzzed, it was Sandra.

"Sorry babe, I hope you are having a wonderful time. I had Bev round here today, dragging that poor mut along. She was furious with Eric, and I suggest he gets in touch to tell her he is safe. Tell him I had managed to calm her down so now is probably a good time to contact her."

John text back, "Having a ball my darling, missing you lots and will pass this onto Eric."

One by one, the rest of the group began to stir. Some with more grace than others. Steve emerged from his room rubbing his eyes, while Danny stumbled out muttering about needing "industrial-strength coffee and a new liver."

Downstairs in the hotel bar, Josh and Peter were already buzzing with energy, clearly unfazed by the day's earlier chaos. Josh was wearing his shades indoors, looking far too pleased with himself, while Peter strutted in holding a giant neon Super Soaker like it was a prized possession.

Steve looked at him, bewildered. "What the hell's that for?" Peter grinned like a man on a mission. "You'll see. I'm locked and loaded, boys—and I suggest you all do the same. It's a water war zone out there!"

He nodded toward the open hotel doors where, just outside, a local street vendor was proudly displaying a whole arsenal of water pistols, foam hats, goggles, and lurid Hawaiian shirts. John pulled Eric to one side and showed him Sandra's text. "Suggest you reach out mate, before it gets serious."

"I'll send her a text now, but then turn my phone off. Don't want her spoiling the night," he said with a grin.

Josh clapped his hands together.

"Right, lads—hydration, mischief, and questionable decisions. Let's go." Armed to the teeth with Super Soakers, water grenades, and questionable sun hats, the lads strutted down the street like a rogue squad of hydration-hungry mercenaries. Josh had strapped two pistols to his belt like a Wild West gunslinger, while Peter carried his oversized cannon like Rambo at a pool party.

Locals and tourists alike were already in full swing. Pickup trucks rumbled past, their backs loaded with giant barrels of water and wild-eyed passengers tossing buckets with reckless abandon. A rogue splash hit Danny square in the chest.

"Oi!" he shouted, spinning around with a grin. "This means war!"

By the time they reached the first bar — barely a hundred yards from the hotel — they were already soaked and laughing like teenagers on the last day of school. The place was chaos in the best possible way. Buckets of water lined the walls, people reloading their weapons and firing at anything that dared move. Music blared from massive speakers, and somewhere in the back, someone was dancing in flippers and a snorkel.

Without missing a beat, Bruce threw his hands in the air. "Twelve beers!" he shouted to the waitress over the madness.

She gave a thumbs-up, expertly dodging a water balloon as she ducked behind the bar. Within moments, twelve ice-cold bottles of Chang were delivered to their soaking-wet table, the condensation dripping like tiny waterfalls in the heat.

Bruce raised his bottle high. "To mayhem, mischief, and absolutely no regrets!"

The boys clinked their beers, water streaming down their faces, shirts stuck to their backs, and not a single dry soul in sight.

"BAAANG-LAAAA, BABY!" Rory's shout cracked across the Phuket night like a gunshot in a monastery. Twelve lads erupted out of the bar like they'd just been released from a pressure cooker — loud, sunburnt, half-pissed, and riding that perfect wave between drunk confidence and terrible decision-making.

The street was thick with heat and chaos. Mopeds buzzed past like angry bees. Vendors shouted about pad Thai, suits, and massages in the same breath. But the lads were on a one-way mission — and that mission was Bangla Road. At the front, Rory strutted like a man who owned the pavement, arms swinging, chin out, t-shirt clinging to a beer belly he wore with pride. Behind him, Bruce slid on a pair of fake Ray-Bans with the swagger of a man convinced they made him bulletproof. Steve, never knowingly underdressed, had strapped on a pair of bright red Speedo swimming goggles — "Mum packed these, and I knew they'd come in handy" — already fogged up despite the fact he was bone dry... for now.

As they hit the corner and turned into the main drag, they fell into formation — twelve across, moving in rhythm, like the least qualified dance troupe Phuket had ever seen. A low-rent Magnificent Seven, but eleven of them and with more body odour and less dignity. They didn't walk — they marched. Heads turning as they passed.

A pair of backpackers paused mid-smoothie, jaws slack. A bar girl snapped a gum bubble and muttered, "Oh no. Another one of these groups." Even a soi dog raised its head, then wisely turned the other way.

Keith started miming finger guns. Eric played air saxophone to music only he could hear. Bruce shouted, "ON TOUR!" so loudly it set off a nearby car alarm.

They were loving it. Feeding off the attention. Grinning like lunatics, pointing at people, high-fiving strangers, soaking in every second of their big Bangla entrance. And then— WHAM! A bucket of freezing cold water hit Rory square in the chest. He froze. Blinked.

"The f*ck was that?!"

Before he could answer himself, another bucket came from the left. Then a hose. Then three kids with neon water pistols appeared from nowhere and unloaded on them like a drive-by at a garden centre. Chaos. Screaming. Squelching. Bruce tried to spin, slipped in his flip-flops, and went down like a folding deckchair. Steve, still in goggles, shouted

"I'M READY!" like he'd trained for this. Dan was hit in the crotch and made a sound no human should ever make.

Within seconds, the swagger was gone. Replaced by twelve dripping men, blinking through wet eyelashes, looking like they'd been dunked in a giant bowl of Thai soup. Laughter erupted from the bars lining the street. Phones came out. Tourists applauded. And standing just ahead, glowing like a beacon of chaos. The Koala Bar! The familiar sprawling, open-air bar with no walls, no rules, and no quiet corners. Music pounded from rattling speakers. Buckets of booze lined the bar top. A woman in tight shorts rang a brass bell and shouted,

"LADY DRINK!" every thirty seconds.
Still soaked, still laughing, the boys staggered forward.

"God, I love this place," Eric muttered, shaking water out of his ear.

Rory, arms outstretched like a wet prophet, grinned:

"Welcome to the f*ckin' jungle, boys." And then the night truly began.

Chapter Thirteen

Grilled Chicken, Hot Birds

The buckets were bottomless, the shots relentless, and the Chang flowed like holy water at a festival for the terminally thirsty. The Koala Bar didn't just have atmosphere — it had weather. The air inside felt humid enough to grow rice. The heat pressed in from all sides, soaked into shirts, and made every forehead glisten like it was auditioning for a bottled water advert. Music thumped from speakers that looked like they'd been bolted to the wall in the early 2000s and had been shaking themselves toward self-destruction ever since. Strobe lights stabbed the darkness, freezing moments in weird, drunken tableaus: a man leaning too far over the bar, a girl laughing with her head thrown back, a waitress carrying six drinks at once with dead-eyed precision.

It wasn't even midnight, but the lads were already six beers past "sensible" and galloping through the kind of manic group energy that thrives on sugar, alcohol, and collective bad judgement. Every round blurred into the next. Nobody was keeping count. Nobody wanted to.

They were surrounded. Each man had at least one girl attached to him like an expensive barnacle — on his lap, curled around his shoulder, or clinking glasses inches from his face. They leaned in close, their perfume mixing with the sweet-sour tang of the drinks, voices pitched to cut through the noise as they delivered the magic words:

"Lady drink?"
"Another one?"
"Two for me and my friend?"
"Bell ring! More fun!"

The "lady drinks" came and went like conjuring tricks — a glass here, an empty stem there — and the boys were too flattered, too dazzled, or too far gone to notice their wallets bleeding out. This wasn't so much a bar bill as it was a slow, expensive mugging wrapped in a smile.

Steve — wearing a pair of mirrored Speedo swim goggles for reasons even he couldn't recall — leaned forward to clink a shot glass with the girl next to him. He missed entirely, the glass glancing off the rim of the ice bucket with a dull thunk.

Ping. His phone lit up.

"Hang on, sweetheart," he muttered, twisting away like he was about to take a classified call. WhatsApp. Suki. The boat date from earlier.

He started stabbing out a reply with the focus of a man defusing a bomb, when Bruce slid in from nowhere and plucked the phone out of his hands.

"Well, well," Bruce said, scanning the screen. "What have we here, then?"

"Give it back!" Steve barked. "Suki's coming here. I like her!"

Bruce raised an eyebrow. "Right. You might find that buffet comes with a few extra dishes, but if it tickles your fancy, crack on, lad. Fill your bloody boots."

He drifted over to Pete, who was caught between a girl in a glittery dress and his own need to wave his arms like he was conducting an orchestra of regret.

"Seems Steve's smitten with the ladyboy," Bruce said casually.

Pete took a thoughtful sip. "Good for him."

"Aye," Bruce grinned. "Can't knock it 'til you've tried it."
They both laughed so hard Pete had to steady himself on the table.

Two seats down, Rory — shirt half-off, grin locked in place — slapped the bar with a flourish and ordered tequila shots for a group of strangers, then promptly forgot who they were for and joined a completely different table.

Then — CLANG! CLANG! CLANG! Josh rang the brass bar bell like it had personally offended him. The place erupted. Girls screamed. Waitresses poured in from every direction. A tsunami of drinks appeared from nowhere, each one a different radioactive shade. Steve leaned toward Craig.

"Welp — that's another 10,000 baht down the drain."

"He can afford it, lucky sod," Craig said, raising his glass. They clinked, as if toasting the soundest investment ever made.

But down at the end of the bar, Keith was miles away. He wasn't thinking about hips or lipstick or whatever giggle Craig was trying to interpret as flirting. He was thinking about food.

The bass rattled his ribs, the air wrapped around him like a damp towel, and his brain locked on one truth: I need grilled chicken. Leaning toward Bruce, he shouted,

"Mate, I'm starving."

Bruce, mid-lap dance from a girl with a Hello Kitty tattoo, gave a limp thumbs up without making eye contact.

Keith pushed back from the table, steadying himself as the floor swayed slightly beneath his feet.

"I'm going to find that grilled chicken guy — the one down the next street. You lot can have the hot birds; I want mine smothered in soy glaze and crispy skin."

Nobody looked up. And so, Keith stepped out into the Phuket night, the noise and neon of the Koala Bar fading behind him. The street hit him like a wave — heat, noise, the smell of exhaust and fried things that probably weren't chicken. Bangla Road roared on to his left, but he turned right into a narrower lane. Here, the light dimmed, the air thickened, and the crowds thinned to pockets of movement: a pair of tourists staggering arm-in-arm, a scooter wobbling under the weight of a family of four, a vendor calling out the price of fake sunglasses.

Keith's shirt was already sticking to his back. His stomach gave a low, insistent grow, then he saw it — the cart. Rusty, paint peeling, haloed by fluorescent bulbs that hummed like lazy bees. Smoke curled up into the night air, carrying the unmistakable perfume of chicken skin blistering over charcoal. The vendor — a man in flip-flops and a faded Manchester United vest — fanned the coals with a battered piece of cardboard, his face shining with heat.

"You come for chicken, my friend?" the man called, flashing a smile full of gaps and survivors.

Keith pointed like a pilgrim recognising a holy relic. "You're the one. You're the bloody chicken guy."

"Very crispy. Very juicy. You want spicy or not spicy?"
Keith considered the question as if it were life or death.

"Spicy. I'm in Thailand. If I don't cry, and my arse doesn't resemble the Japanese flag tomorrow, it's not authentic."
The vendor laughed, slapping the grill with his tongs.

"OK, my friend! One spicy chicken for you. You want rice or just chicken?"

"Rice is for sober people," Keith said. "Just give me the meat."

He paid in crumpled baht, tipped generously, and lowered himself into a red plastic chair that wobbled dangerously under his weight. Traffic whined past. Scooters zipped by like angry insects. Somewhere nearby, a drunk Russian couple argued over a banana pancake. Keith leaned back, half-closing his eyes as the scent from the grill wrapped around him like a greasy embrace.

"This," he whispered, "is what living tastes like."

The vendor chuckled.

"You eat now. Then go back to Bangla for more lady problem."

Keith grinned. "Mate, right now, this chicken's the only bird I can handle."

The first bite was a small epiphany — skin shattering between his teeth, meat tender and smoky, the chili sauce detonating in his sinuses. He closed his eyes, chewing slowly, savouring every moment. Grease dripped onto his chin; he caught it with his tongue like a man who knew what mattered. Halfway through, a scooter purred to a stop beside the cart. Two girls hopped off — both in tiny denim shorts, one dusted with glitter across her collarbones, the other with a phoenix tattoo climbing out of a cocktail glass. They chatted with the vendor in Thai, glancing at Keith with amused curiosity.

Keith looked up at the tattooed one. "Bloody hell, you're gorgeous. Almost as fabulous as this chicken."

They giggled. The phoenix girl tilted her head.

"You handsome man. You want to have sexy fun? On the beach maybe?"

Keith blinked. "Wait, what? On the beach?" He paused. "How much are we talkin' here? Chicken's not the only thing on a budget."

"Two thousand baht. Short time. You lucky man. We bring the party.

Keith scratched his head. "One girl or both?"

"Only me," she said, pointing to herself. "She drive home."
He nodded, sobering slightly, the heat of the chili sauce working overtime on his imagination.

"Alright," he said, tossing his chicken skewer onto the plate like a man closing a deal. "But I want a sea view."

She grabbed his hand. "Come, sexy chicken man."

They walked across the road, shoes in hand, stepping through the thin trees to the quiet, darkened beach where only the sound of gentle waves and distant bar music remained. Most sunbeds were empty. They found one — tilted back, a little sandy, and barely holding together.

She straddled him, giggling as he leaned back, wide-eyed, a mix of surprise, curry burps and absolute disbelief.
He muttered, "This trip is un-bloody-real."

As the waves lapped gently behind them, and the moonlight bounced off her glittery shoulders, Keith gave himself over to the madness — awkwardly, hilariously, like a man who only came for grilled meat but got served something entirely different. Keith sank further into the sunbed with a grunt, legs akimbo, shirt clinging to him like clingfilm to a Sunday roast. His new friend turned him over, and laid back with the smooth confidence of someone who'd done this before, giggling as she flicked her hair and adjusted herself. Keith looked down, eyes half-lidded, a ridiculous grin on his face. You've still got it, my son, he thought. Phuket's answer to Magic Mike… if Mike had a dad bod and a dodgy knee.

The waves lapped lazily nearby. A soft breeze drifted over them. The stars sparkled like they were in on the joke. Keith was in full swing, half performance, half gamble, when—
Tap. Tap.
A hand. On his shoulder.
He froze.

The girl paused, confused. Keith craned his neck around — part curiosity, part panic — expecting the police, a beach dog, or worse: one of the lads with a camera. Instead, standing over him, calm as a monk in a rave, was a tall African man, beaming from ear to ear. He wore cargo shorts, a tie-dye Bob Marley tee, and carried a large basket filled with mangoes.

"Mango, my friend?" the man asked, as if he were offering a handshake at a business lunch.

Keith stared, mouth open, brain buffering. The girl looked at the man, then at Keith, then let out a snort of laughter.
Keith blinked.

"Mate... really?"

The man just smiled wider. "Fresh and sweet. Very good for power, my friend. Keeps you strong."

Keith looked at the girl. She shrugged.
"No thank you," Keith mumbled. "Bit of a... weird time."

The mango man replied. "Mango makes you big strong boy, better than Viagra!"

Keith sighed, slightly derailed, then turned back to the task at hand. A few minutes later, things wrapped up as awkwardly and hilariously as they began.
He sat up, straightening his shirt, still sweating like a butcher in a sauna. He reached into his pocket and passed her a folded-up wad of baht.

"Thanks," he said, with a grin that was half charm, half confusion.

"You strong man," she said, pocketing the notes. "Very funny too."

Keith nodded, already wondering how the hell he was going to explain this to the others.

By the time Keith stumbled back into the Koala Bar, the place was buzzing. The music seemed even louder, the lady drinks were flowing, and the lads were now deep in a cocktail of shots, beer, and delusion. Steve was trying to dance with Suki, but he was using her more as a leaning post, than a smooching dance. Craig was in a deep conversation with a waitress about Man City, or Man Utd's chances this season, even though she thought "Pep" was a dessert.

Keith approached the table like a man returning from battle — shirt half-untucked, hair windswept, and the unmistakable swagger of someone who'd just had an adventure.

Bruce spotted him first. "Oi, oi! Look what the cat dragged back."

Eric turned, saw Keith's grin and his slightly dishevelled state. "Bloody hell, mate. What was in the chicken, you look like you've been in a wind tunnel made of regret."

Keith slapped a hand on the table, dropped into a chair, and took a long swig from Bruce's beer without asking.

"You are not going to believe what just happened," he said, wiping his mouth.
Bruce leaned in. "Tell me everything."

Keith launched in, arms waving like he was describing a UFO landing.

"So, there I am, on the beach, sunbed barely holding together, I'm on top, we're going at it — it's all happening. I'm thinking to myself: this is it, Keithy boy. You've peaked. You're like Bond… if Bond was sweaty and covered in chicken grease."

Eric cackled. "Please tell me someone filmed this."

Keith shook his head. "Thankfully not, there was no time for cameras, mate. I'm mid-thrust — peak performance — when I feel this tap on my shoulder."

The lads leaned in.

"I turn around, thinking it's the cops, or worse — one of you twats with your phone — and there's this guy standing there. Massive bloke. Smiling like he's just been told he's won the lottery."

Bruce raised an eyebrow. "Wait… what?"

Keith held up a hand. "Basket of mangoes. I kid you not. Just standing there, on the beach, during the act, offering me bloody mangoes."

Eric was howling now. "Did he want a tip or just thought it was snack time?"

"I don't know!" Keith said. "He's there like, 'Mango, my friend? Very fresh. Good for energy.' Like it's the most normal thing in the world to interrupt a seaside shag with a bloody fruit platter."

Bruce wiped tears from his eyes. "So, what did you say?"

Keith paused, slowly reached into a plastic bag at his side, and with the straightest face possible, held up two perfectly ripe mangoes. "Anyone fancy a mango?"

The table exploded. Chairs tipped back, drinks sloshed, someone knocked over a bucket of ice. Even the bar girls were laughing, having no idea why, but caught up in the infectious madness.

Keith sat back, smug as ever, holding up his tropical prize like a gladiator presenting his spoils. And just like that, the legend of the Mango Man was born.

Chapter Fourteen

Three Men and a Soapy

The alarms buzzed in unison; a discordant symphony of regret composed entirely of dial-up modem screeches and Barry Manilow's "Copacabana." In Bruce's room, the device emitted a shrill, persistent shriek a sound he associated with angry ex-wives, and crazy music teachers. Without opening his eyes, Bruce's hand, guided by muscle memory honed over decades of avoiding responsibility, snaked out from under the covers, located the snooze button with pinpoint accuracy, and slammed it down.

A blessed silence settled over the room. He exhaled, the scent of stale beer, faint lemongrass, and a lingering hint of "eau de regret" clinging to his breath and burrowed deeper into the pillows. Sleep was a precious commodity, and he wasn't about to let some arbitrary schedule rob him of it. Besides, Lakeside Palms could wait. His liver, on the other hand, was staging a full-blown revolt. Across the hall, the situation was far more dire. Eric's alarm was met with a series of violent retches that sounded like a badger giving birth to a washing machine being punted down a staircase. He lurched out of bed, stumbled toward the bathroom, and unleashed another torrent of gastric misery into the toilet bowl a technicolour eruption that featured chunks of everything he'd consumed in the past 72 hours, including, he suspected, a rogue cocktail umbrella. When the heaving subsided, he reached for his phone, his face pale and clammy, his hair stuck to his forehead like seaweed.

Eric (7:15 AM): "Lads, giving it a miss today. Think I ate something bad. Feeling rough as a badger's arse. Seriously, I think I just saw my own spleen."

The replies came quickly, dripping with thinly veiled schadenfreude:

John (7:16 AM): "Oh, of course, Eric. Nothing to do with the fifteen gallons of Chang you consumed yesterday! Or was it the 'special' spring rolls from that bloke with one tooth?" 😂

Danny (7:17 AM): "Yeah, and the mystery meat skewers... and the questionable green sauce... Don't forget the deep-fried grasshoppers! Honestly, mate, you eat like a bloody locust. Get well soon, though. More birdies for us!"

Eric groaned, his stomach churning at the mere mention of food, and tossed the phone onto the bedside table. A gentle day on the links, or even a gentle day breathing, was impossible.

Meanwhile, back in Keith's room, a different kind of excuse was brewing – one seasoned with equal parts melodrama and Bengay. He stirred, wincing as a familiar ache pulsed through his lower back, a symphony of creaks and groans emanating from his spine. Years of questionable posture, dodgy sunbeds, carrying the emotional weight of his failed Tinder dates, and that incident with the overly enthusiastic limbo dancer had taken their toll. Golf was supposed to be relaxing, not a medieval torture device. Besides, he'd pulled something last night trying to show Suki how to do the YMCA.

Keith (7:20 AM): "Back's gone again, lads. Seriously seized up. Gonna have to give Lakeside Palms a miss. Enjoy the course and try not to slice any balls into the jungle. I'm not fit enough to go searching, or even swing today." He grimaced, rolling gingerly to his side, as if the very act of turning might snap something vital.

The replies were, surprisingly, sympathetic this time:

John (7:21 AM): "Ah, bad luck mate. You're falling apart faster than a cheap suitcase. Rest up! We'll bring you back a souvenir... maybe a bottle of that tiger balm stuff?"

Danny (7:21 AM): "Take it easy Keith, those fairways will still be here. Unlike your vertebrae. 😂"

Meanwhile, at Lakeside Palms. As the minibus pulled up, Craig took to the first tee once again as he was looking as bright as could be. There as well was Stu and the rivalry between the two of them seemed even more fierce today as they had been locked in a dead tight competition all week.

After some friendly heckling amongst the other lads, Danny teed up the ball and watched with a wry smile as Steve went for one of his now famous hooks at a ball that had ended up near the lakes and was close to the edge of the water.

"Be careful with this one mate there's a water hazard and I don't think I brought any spares" screamed Steve's long-time pal, John; after a mighty swing however, he swung himself into the lake. With a yell of frustration, he threw his club at the ball, in a flailing motion that sent it spinning wildly into the trees, whilst also sending himself careering ass over tit into the water screaming

"Oh for god's sake!".

Shouting to the boys, with water running down his face, "I'm off back to the club house lads, think I've pulled something" "Think I'll come with you my hangover is so bad at the moment," said Bernard. The other boys carried on in the sunshine without another thought for either of them.

John watched Steve's retreating figure then shouted ""make sure you buy that towel you muppet, a nice souvenir for you!" As Steve limped toward the clubhouse, Bernie ambled beside him, a grin plastered on his face. "Well, that was a bloody disaster. Still, at least the sun's out. Shame to waste a perfectly good day."

They trudged through the entrance, leaving a trail of muddy footprints on the freshly mopped floor. The scent of air conditioning and stale coffee hung in the air, a welcome respite from the oppressive heat and humidity of the course.

Steve made a beeline for the pro shop, dripping water with every step. Two young women behind the counter looked up, their eyes widening in amusement as he approached.

"Oh dear, sir, what happened to you?" one of them asked, stifling a giggle.

Steve turned and gestured vaguely toward the course, leaving a spray of droplets in his wake. "I fell into that lake over there. It was a valiant attempt at a heroic recovery shot, but alas, I ended up becoming one with the local ecosystem. Also, I think a fish might have nibbled my arse."

The women dissolved into laughter. "Oh no, that's terrible!" one of them managed to say between giggles. "Well, let's get you some dry clothes, sir. We can't have you catching your death."

And with that, the ladies sprang into action, bustling around Steve like a pair of overly enthusiastic pit crew members. One produced a fluffy towel, while the other started rummaging through the clothing racks. Steve stood there, bewildered but not entirely displeased, as they fussed over him, leaving a small puddle on the changing room floor.

Bernie leaned against a nearby display of golf balls, watching the scene with a bemused smile. "You know," he said to no one in particular, "I haven't seen a woman this keen to undress a man since that bird from Doncaster on my stag do... in 1978."

One of the pro shop assistants turned to Bernie "Can I help you with anything sir?" Bernie smiled and said "As much as I enjoy watching a woman keen to undress a man, I'll skip this. Is there a massage service here?"

"Yes, sir," she replied, pointing toward a discreet staircase, "Head over to the spa at the resort upstairs. They offer a full range of treatments. I'm sure they can sort you out."

Bernie thanked her and headed for the stairs, a spring returning to his step. He was a simple man. Golf had failed him this day, but a luxurious pampering session never did.

Upstairs, the spa was a haven of tranquillity — soft lighting, calming music, and the scent of exotic oils hanging in the air. A serene-looking woman with a gentle smile greeted him and led him toward the changing rooms.

"Please make yourself comfortable, sir," she said, handing him a neatly folded pile of clothes. "Your therapist will be with you shortly."

Bernie entered the changing room and blinked. On the bench lay a pair of black, net-like pants that resembled something between a fishnet stocking and a net. He picked them up gingerly, holding them to the light.

"Good God," he muttered to himself, "If I put these on, my tackle will look like a frozen shrimp caught in a kids fishing net?"

With a sigh and a grin, Bernie wriggled into the "pants," discreetly adjusting his anatomy to avoid any unfortunate snags. He emerged from the changing room and was promptly led to a dimly lit treatment room, where a soothing Thai melody played softly. The fabric scratched faintly against his skin, making him wonder if the netting was actually intended for seafood storage.

For the next hour, Bernie was in heaven. The therapist worked wonders, her skilled hands kneading away knots and tension he hadn't realized he was carrying. He drifted into a state of blissful semi-consciousness as she moved from a facial to a full body massage to a foot rub, each treatment expertly executed and designed to relax every muscle and fibre in his being. This wasn't the chaotic, potentially dodgy "tickle" he'd envisioned earlier. This was something altogether different, something... dare he say it... therapeutic.

As the massage drew to a close, Bernie stretched languidly and let out a contented sigh. He felt like a new man.

The afternoon sunlight filtered through the curtains, casting lazy patterns on the floor, as Bruce stirred awake. The clock read 1:30 PM, and Bruce blinked groggily, his mind slowly registering the missed morning of golf. He glanced over at his phone, a piece of technology he normally tried to ignore until lunch, and found a slew of messages from the morning's chaos.

Bruce sat up, yawning, and typed out a quick text to his two friends, wondering if they too had survived their alarms without feeling like they had been through a blender.

Bruce (1:32 PM): "Afternoon, lads. Did we collectively decide sleep was more eventful than golf? How's everyone feeling?"

Almost instantly, replies came:

Eric (1:33 PM): "Woke up feeling like I've spent the night wrestling with badgers, but alive! Definitely skipped the golf adventure. What about our next move?"

Keith (1:34 PM): "I'm about as mobile as a stack of bricks, so golf was off the table. However, I have a suggestion to elevate our day!"
Bruce's interest was piqued.

Bruce (1:35 PM): "Go on, then. What's the idea?" His curiosity was piqued, picturing all sorts of mad possibilities.

Keith replied with enthusiasm, despite the implied aches and pains.

Keith (1:36 PM): "Remember that building near the beach. Justine's something-or-other? It's a well-known Soapy place. I say we give ourselves a fun, relaxing treat!"

Bruce chuckled. The idea of an afternoon spent indulging in a bit of comical mischief was far too tempting to pass up.

Bruce (1:37 PM): "I'm game! Nothing quite like a Soapy to wash away the woes of missing out on golf."

Eric quickly jumped on board, feeling his spirits lift at the thought of a laugh to lighten the day's fiascos.

Eric (1:38 PM): "Count me in. Let's meet at the bar in five, gather our wits and head over. It's high time we see what all the fuss is about!"

With a plan in place, the trio shook off the remnants of their morning lethargy and prepared to embrace the unexpected adventure that awaited. This Soapy promised laughter and, a story to tell the boys later—a much more enticing prospect than hacking away at Lakeside Palms ever was. They might have missed their tee times, but this was the kind of day that memories (and probably exaggerated stories) were made of.

The boys hit the streets, freshly showered and ready for their impromptu spa adventures, and immediately found themselves under attack. Super soakers appeared out of nowhere, squirting water with the enthusiasm of kids at a birthday party. Bruce, Eric, and Keith yelped and ducked, trying to dodge the spray while making their way toward Justine's—aka, the legendary Soapy spot.

"Run for your lives!" Bruce shouted, shaking his fist at his attackers, who retaliated with a fresh blast of water to the face. "This is worse than the time I got caught in a rainstorm during a picnic!"

Finally reaching the steps of Justine's, they paused, dripping and panting, to catch their breath. As they bravely stepped forward through the soaked chaos, they were greeted by a gentleman standing at the entrance, who looked like he'd stepped right out of a travel brochure—an overly friendly smile spreading across his face.

"Are you here for the treatment?" he asked eagerly in a thick Thai accent, eyes twinkling with a mix of curiosity and mischief.

The boys nodded as if it was the most obvious thing in the world, trying to wipe water out of their eyes.

"Excellent," he said with a grin. "Follow me, gentlemen."

He led them to the end of an oddly decorated room, where a large window was sliced into three sections. Behind the glass, they saw rows of women sitting in perfect symmetry—each one level above the last, stacked five layers deep like a bizarre, glamorous pyramid. They looked up at the scene, a mixture of curiosity and bewilderment.

"The ones on the left," the man explained, "are our most affordable, slightly older, very good, but not quite as attractive as the others." He paused dramatically. "That's 2,500 baht."
He pointed to the middle section. "These are younger, more attractive, and a little more—shall we say—premium," he said suavely. "That's 3,500 baht."

Finally, he gestured to the right. "And these," he said with a wink, "are our top-tier service. The best of the best. Cost a bit more—5,000 baht—but totally worth it." He looked at the boys, who were trying to process what they were seeing without burst of laughter.
"Now, take a moment," he continued kindly. "Mae will get you something to drink. Think about your choices. Come back when you're ready."

Eric stared at the scene, then shook his head. "Bloody hell," he muttered, giving the window a suspicious look. Without warning, he turned and strolled right into it, as if he'd forgotten there was glass there. His forehead hit the pane with a loud thwack, leaving a red imprint, while the girls behind the glass burst into laughter. Bruce and Keith just looked at each other, eyes wide, then burst into uncontrollable giggles.

"Remind me not to let Eric choose the 'premium' option," Bruce muttered through his laughter, as Eric mumbled and rubbed his forehead like he'd just been hit with a clue.

Meanwhile, the staff behind the glass kept giggling—probably wondering if these were their future customers. Bruce (with dramatic tension): "In... three... two... one...! I suggest we go two from the top, and one from the bottom—that's yours Eric, the man of... shall we say, particular taste."

They all chuckled, imagining Eric's legendary pick. With their selections made and a good dose of laughter, the trio headed off with their companions, each trying to pretend they weren't secretly nervous. The 90-minute session felt like an eternity, but eventually, they all reassembled in the foyer, dripping dry, grinning like a bunch of kids who had just escaped detention.

Outside, the hot sun hit them like a frying pan as they headed down the street. Keith, ever the philosopher of misadventures, turned to his friends with a wry smile.

Keith: "So, boys… how was it for you?" He raised an eyebrow, a mischievous grin spreading across his face.

Bruce, wiping his hands on his shorts, beamed.

"Excellent," he said. "I've never felt so clean—and yet so filthy—at the same time. It's like I've just been born again, but someone forgot to tell me I'm also a mess."

They burst into uncontrollable laughter, the sheer absurdity of the day catching up with them. As they continued walking, Bruce pulled out his phone and quickly WhatsApp the group.

Bruce (texting): "Me, Eric, and Keith are already out. Meet you all at the Koala Bar when you're done with golf. Let's make this a night to remember...or forget."

The group picture—full of grinning, soaked, slightly traumatized but thoroughly entertained – blinked onto the screen, anticipation building.

Later that evening, the boys finally regrouped at the Koala Bar—their home, from home this week. The night kicked off with a flurry of laughter, shots, and stories. Eric, barely able to contain himself, shared the tale of his accidental "treatment" at Justine's—details exaggerated and animated, wide-eyed with comedic horror.

Everyone listened with rapt attention, some with grimaces, others with giggles, as Eric mimed walking face-first into the glass, rubbing his forehead with exaggerated flair. In the dim glow of neon lights, the group's chaos only grew. There were silly dances, questionable karaoke performances, and more than a few questionable decisions. They toasted to the day— missed golf, happy misadventures, and stories that would be retold for years to come.

And as the night wore on, so did the jokes, the drinks, and the camaraderie—proof that sometimes the best days are the ones you never planned, especially when they involve an unexpected "treatment," a lot of laughter, and a night of pure, glorious mayhem.

Chapter Fifteen

Fore the Last Time

The alarm went off like a bomb in Steve's room — shrill, relentless, and about as welcome as a wasp in a wetsuit. Honestly, if the snooze button had been a person, Steve would have been up on charges. He groaned, face down in a pillow that smelled suspiciously of coconut lotion, tequila, and something that definitely wasn't his deodorant. Next to him, Suki lay curled up, snoring softly, one leg draped across him like she'd claimed him in some kind of sleep-based international marriage ceremony.

Steve blinked. His vision was foggy. That could've been the Chang… or the fact that he was still wearing his Speedo swimming goggles around his neck.

He kissed Suki gently on the forehead, like a confused prince waking up a beachside Cinderella, then rolled out of bed and sauntered to the bathroom, humming the Rocky theme tune under his breath and completely nude except for one sock.

In the next room, Bruce was waking up in a different sort of fairytale — more Hansel and Hangover. He was curled in the foetal position, surrounded by empty crisp packets, a crumpled 7-Eleven toastie half-glued to his chest like a greasy badge of honour. One flip-flop was on the ceiling fan. He squinted at the daylight, hissed like a vampire, then reached for a bottle of water and missed, knocking it under the bed.

"Brilliant," he croaked. "Hydration's overrated anyway." Groaning like a pensioner doing yoga, he shuffled toward the shower with all the grace of a dying giraffe.

Meanwhile, across the hall, Bernard's alarm chirped cheerfully like it had no idea what kind of chaos it was waking. He stirred. Blinked. Looked left… then right. He was in bed with two stunning Thai women, both fast asleep, tangled in sheets and glitter. A single sandal was hanging off the bedside lamp. His left nipple had a lipstick mark on it. The bedside table held a used condom wrapper, a half-empty bottle of water, and a strip of Viagra, the top three tablets now gone. Bernard grinned.

"Still got it," he whispered to himself, like he'd just won the Masters.

He sat up — slowly. His knees cracked. His back popped. His stomach rumbled with ominous intent. He looked in the bathroom mirror, there was a Viagra tablet stuck between his eyes like a bindi. Kin' ell (as they say in the Queen's dodgy cousin's English), he thought to himself. Must have been a hell of a night! Then — a fart. A titanic, floorboard-shaking, confidence-killing fart erupted from deep within. It echoed through the room like a ship's horn announcing its departure.

One of the girls stirred, blinked, then turned to him in the bathroom and shouted

"Big sexy boy! You want to try again now?"

Bernard paused, trying to decide if he still had a second round in him… then felt a twinge in his hip. "Maybe not stallion," he muttered. "More… cart horse." With a proud shuffle, he headed to the shower, still grinning. A true veteran.

Already at the Blue Mountain driving range — unshaven, unsteady, but deadly serious — were Stu and Craig. They hadn't spoken much that morning. This was not the time for jokes. This was war. On the surface, it was just another pristine country club driving range, nestled in well-manicured grounds, and a family of sunbathing stray dogs watching in confusion. But for Stu and Craig, it was Augusta. It was St. Andrews. It was the final showdown for the coveted, made-up, and entirely pointless title of Phuket Champion. Craig stood tall, exuding an unearned level of elegance — like a man in a deodorant commercial. He adjusted his glove, eyed up the range, and let rip a majestic drive. It soared into the humid sky, dead straight, long, and smooth as butter. Stu watched it land. Silently. Deadpan. Jealous. Then he stepped up and sliced his own drive so far right it nearly took out a man buying iced tea on the main road.

He didn't flinch. He just muttered,

"Bit of fade."

Craig didn't say a word. He just smiled slightly. The smug, irritating smile of a man who'd clearly had a proper breakfast, a proper sleep, and probably hadn't shagged anyone in a beach bar at 3 a.m.

Stu teed up another ball, glancing sideways at Craig like it was a Wild West duel. He took a deep breath, tried to focus, and swung hard — too hard — sending the ball dribbling ten yards along the mat.

"Practice swing," he grunted.

Craig responded by launching another gorgeous arc into the morning air, turning slightly mid-swing to say,

"You feeling the pressure, champ?"

Stu's jaw clenched. "Just warming up, mate. You'll see."
He looked around for moral support — but all he saw was Bernard arriving in flip-flops and a floral shirt, carrying his clubs like a man arriving at a barbecue, not a sporting event.

Behind him, Steve, still wearing his swim goggles like a helmet, stumbled up and yelled, "Right lads — who's ready to completely f*** this course up?!"

From a bench nearby, Rory shouted back,

"Haven't sobered up since Tuesday, mate, let's do this!"

But for Stu and Craig, it was still just the two of them. Craig rolled another ball onto the mat and looked up with that god-awful twinkle in his eye.

"Fore the Last Time, eh?"

Stu cracked his neck. "This ain't over." He stepped up to the mat, focused, breathed in the thick Phuket air, and swung. The ball made solid contact. It rose. It held its line. It sailed out majestically. And then, with tragic inevitability, it clipped a passing power line, bounced off a bird, and dropped dead in the bushes. Stu sighed.

Craig clapped, slow and sarcastic. "Well struck. Real championship stuff."

Stu turned to him.

"Hope you fall in a bunker and meet a snake."

Craig smiled. The battle had begun. Stu and Craig stared each other down like two cowboys at high noon — only sweatier, pinker, and slightly hungover. But before a club could be raised in fury, Bruce called out from behind the tee box, beer already in hand.

"Alright lads — group photo time! One last glorious memory before we all shank our way through this tropical hellscape!"

The boys gathered slowly — each holding their drivers, fixing their shirts, and trying to remember which end of the club they were meant to hold. One by one, they lined up across the first tee box, twelve men in various shades of sunburn and disrepair. Golf caps backwards. Tummy rolls out. Eyes squinting against the Phuket glare. They looked like a boyband reunion tour no one had asked for — a cross between Ocean's Twelve and a stag-do for the hopelessly divorced.

"Let's get the caddies in!" shouted Bruce, motioning like a game show host. The caddies — twelve cheerful Thai women in wide-brimmed hats and bright shirts — trotted over and knelt in front of the boys, all grinning as if this were a wedding photo and not the start of something resembling a slapstick war movie.

"Would you look at that," said Eric, passing his phone to the starter who was eager to take the shot. "The Magnificent Twelve, riding one last time."

"More like the Sweaty Dozen," muttered Steve, adjusting his goggles.

Bruce raised his beer like a medieval knight.

"To bad decisions, sunstroke, and losing at least three balls a hole!"

"Phuket forever!" someone shouted from the back.

With that, they dispersed to their respective tee shots — a collection of strutting, stretching, and more than one poorly-timed fart Bernard was up first. Still riding high from the previous night's escapades, and with an air of misplaced confidence that could only come from Viagra and victory, he stepped up to the tee like Tiger Woods in 2005. He took two practice swings, without a club — both wildly different in speed and technique — then stepped back.

His caddie handed him a driver. He nodded solemnly, squinted down the fairway, and unleashed a swing so wide and fast it looked like he was trying to remove a bee from his shoulder. The ball sliced violently right. Not a fade. Not a draw. A pure, unfiltered, 90-degree rocket into the trees. There was a small rustle. Then silence.

"Think it opened up over there," Bernard said hopefully.
His caddie, standing perfectly still, stared at the trees with narrowed eyes.

"No," she said in perfect English. "That's gone."

Bernard started marching toward the jungle like a man going after a lost dog, but the caddie put a hand on his arm and shook her head.

"I saw where it land. Ball near tree. Tree have snake. Big one."
Bernard paused. He weighed his options: bravery, stupidity, or a cold beer instead.
"A snake?"
She nodded.
"Cobra?"
"Maybe. Could be python. Could be angry."

He looked toward the brush, then back at the fairway, then back at the brush. Then the caddie simply said,

"Drop one. That's unplayable."

The other lads burst out laughing. Eric started slow clapping. Even the caddies had to hide behind their visors to keep from snorting beer out their noses.

"Mate, when even the locals are telling you to quit — you know it's bad."

"I've had worse," said Bernard, reaching for another ball.

"At least the snake didn't ask if I wanted a mango." Shouted Craig.

Next up, Rory swung with such force he spun himself off the tee box and landed on his arse, narrowly missing his caddie. Pete hit his ball so low it skipped three times off the cart path and nearly took out a squirrel. Steve, still partially steamed from last night and wearing his shirt backwards, shanked his into a pond and blamed his chakras.

By the time Stu stepped up, the caddies were trading bets in Thai on which player would finish with the fewest clubs still intact. Craig watched him carefully, arms folded, chewing gum like a smug assassin. Stu gripped his club like a man strangling a snake and swung......only to top it thirty yards into a muddy patch just short of the ladies' tees. No one said a word. Then Bruce coughed and muttered, "Textbook!"

Craig stepped up and absolutely smoked one down the middle. Perfect flight. Perfect balance. The sound of the strike was like thunder. Stu watched in silent rage, gripping his club harder than ever. As the group moved down the fairway, twelve men, twelve caddies, six cool boxes of beer, and a golf cart that smelled like hashish den, they looked less like golfers and more like a travelling circus. But they were in it together. One last round. One last disaster. One last go at Phuket glory. One last excuse to call themselves athletes while drinking more than a rugby club on tour. They were sunburnt. They were hungover. They were terrible at golf.

But they were alive. And for now, that was enough. By the time they made the turn at the 10th tee, the air was heavy with humidity, regret, and the faint smell of fermented Chang sweat. Half the lads were already in trouble. Bernard had lost four balls, two gloves, and a caddie who

"Needed a break."

Pete was playing barefoot after claiming his shoes were

"Suffocating his soul."

Rory had somehow convinced a local kid to caddie for him in exchange for a packet of Oreos. And Bruce was lying on the 9th green, swearing blind he could feel the Earth rotating.
But none of that mattered.
Because the real battle was just heating up.

Stu vs. Craig. Nine holes left. All square. Pride, beers, and the title of Phuket Golf Champion on the line.

Hole 10 – Par 4 – The Banana Dawg

Craig striped his tee shot down the middle with a majestic baby draw. Stu answered back with a low stinger that chased down the fairway like a dog after a sausage.

"Game on," muttered Bruce, eating a bao bun.

Craig hit the green in two and two-putted for par. Stu drained a 10-footer to match.

"Never in doubt," he said, casually blowing a kiss to his caddie, who blushed and gave him a thumbs-up — or possibly a signal to slow down.

Hole 11 – Par 3 – The Island Tease

Pete tried to tee off with a sand wedge and a can of Leo beer in one hand. It ended predictably.

The contest ahead was getting really serious, Craig landed his ball pin-high, eight feet from the flag. Stu plopped his about five feet closer. Craig missed his birdie. Stu drained his.

"That's one," Stu said, casually checking his cuticles like he wasn't about to combust with competitive joy.

Hole 12 – The Beer Cart Incident

On the 12th tee, Rory drove his ball into the beer cart — after bribing the caddie — and rolled it straight into a bunker, taking out three clubs, two beers, and one innocent lizard.

Meanwhile, Stu hit his tee shot long and straight. Craig, unfazed, bombed his 3-wood to within chipping distance. Then, with the finesse of a Michelin-star chef flipping an egg, Craig chipped in from the fringe. Eagle! Stu was on the edge of the green and chipped to within 2 inches of the hole.

"How the hell do you do that; you make it look so easy" Steve asked.

"You need to choke down the shaft a little more" replied Stu

"That's exactly what I said to that bird last night" replied Bruce as he walked off laughing.

"Back to level, sunshine," he smirked, walking off like he owned the fairway.

Hole 13 – The Noodle Swing

Steve, still with goggles around his neck, tried to drive with a 9-iron. His ball went backwards.

"Must be the altitude," he muttered, before ordering more Chang. Back in the land of competence, Craig and Stu both made par. The match remained locked. They didn't talk much now — just nods, smirks, and the occasional sarcastic clap.

Hole 14 – Par 5 – Trouble Brewing

Bernard drove his ball into a tree, and while retrieving it, got stung on the arse by a wasp.

"Nature is attacking me!" he shouted, running in circles while a caddie sprayed him with what may have been mosquito repellent or coconut oil.

Stu made birdie with a sublime third shot over a palm tree. Craig answered with a laser-beamed approach and drained his putt. Still level.

Hole 15 – Things Get Serious

They both birdied. No jokes. No distractions. Even Bruce stopped narrating his life story to a baffled caddie just to watch them.

Hole 16 – Par 3 – Chaos Returns

As Craig lined up his putt, Pete let off a party popper behind him, causing Craig to flinch and push his shot wide. Stu laughed so hard he nearly fell over — until his own putt lipped out.

"Call it even?" Craig asked.
"Phuket, why not."

Hole 17 – Craig's Glory

Craig hit a towering drive, stiffed his wedge, and drained the putt. One up, one to play.

Hole 18 – The Clutch Finish

Stu knew he needed magic. And he summoned it. A towering tee shot, a majestic second shot that landed six feet from the pin. Craig was on the green too, but further back. He putted first... and left it short. Stu looked up, then down. He lined it up, breathed deep, and dropped it centre cup. Birdie. All square.

The round ended in sweaty handshakes and explosive applause from the gallery — most of whom had no idea what had happened. Back on the 18th green, Stu and Craig raised their clubs in salute.

"Tied," said Craig. "No one wins."

"No one ever does, mate — but we keep pretending anyway," Stu replied with a grin. They fist-bumped. Then hugged.

Then Bruce shouted,

"Right boys, tonight is the last ride out, let's get absolutely ruined!"

Chapter Sixteen

Last Tango in Bangla

The minibus rattled back into Patong just before sunset, clattering to a halt outside the hotel like an overstuffed piñatas of sweat, clubs, and sunburnt egos. No one said much at first. It wasn't exhaustion — they were well beyond that. This was something else. That subtle pause when a great thing starts to feel like it's winding down. But not yet. Bruce clapped his hands.

"Right, lads. One more feed before the mayhem. Market street. Ten minutes."

The boys didn't argue, they all simply went straight to the bar. After a few beers, they made their way around the corner from the hotel to that little chaotic, beautiful street market — a riot of sizzling woks, clattering ladles, neon signs, and the kind of smells that made you question whether you'd ever tasted real food before in your life. Pad Thai crackled in hot oil, noodles tossed high with bean sprouts and a dash of fire. Green curry simmered in great bubbling cauldrons, steam rising into the night like aromatic smoke signals. It was less a cooking sound and more a drumroll for the feast of bad decisions to come.

Skewers of chicken, pork, even things they couldn't identify, turned slowly over charcoal grills, popping and spitting like they had a vendetta.

Plastic tables lined the pavement, ice-cold Singhas appeared without asking, and the boys tucked in like men possessed. Craig was double-fisting Pad Thai and a spicy papaya salad like a man on death row. Rory tackled a green curry so hot he looked like he was having a religious experience. Pete, for reasons no one understood, ordered frog and said it tasted

"like chicken, from the sea."

It was glorious — the kind of glorious that made you want to write home, but only in emojis. Even Steve, completely smitten with the thoughts of seeing Suki again, managed to inhale a bowl of noodles while claiming he could taste

"the notes of coriander through the steam barrier."

Then Bruce stood up. He held his beer like a microphone, cleared his throat, and in that rarest of moments — the entire group went quiet.

"Lads," he began, looking around at the eleven battered, boozy, magnificent idiots, who had somehow made it through a week of sun, golf, and social destruction. "What a trip." There was a brief clink of bottles. Heads nodded. "We've played golf like maniacs. Some of us worse than others—" (Bernard raised his hand proudly) "—and some of us like it was the bloody PGA Tour. Stu. Craig. You two mad bastards brought the drama. You played like pros... until Pete accidentally putted into your line from the bunker."

Laughter rolled across the table. Bruce took a breath. His tone shifted.

"But it's more than golf, isn't it? More than hangovers and... ping pong balls and... well, let's not name everything."

A pause. Even the beer girl slowed her pouring.

"This week... this week's been something we didn't know we needed. All of us, every bloody last one of you marvellous buggers!"

A quiet murmur of agreement.

"This trip for me especially. You all know the car crash I've been through in my divorce, and I thank each and every one of you for being there for me, in the darkest times. We left jobs, stress, emails, wives, Tinder disasters—" (Steve choked on his beer) "—and for seven days, we were just the lads again. Just... us. No filters. No clocks. No plans beyond the next tee box or beer." He raised his bottle. "I'll go back to an empty flat next week," he said softly. "Some of you will go back to the chaos of kids and reality. But I swear to God, when I'm sitting there eating beans on toast, I'll be smiling. Because I'll remember this week. This stupid, messy, beautiful week."

He paused. Then:

"To the Brotherhood of the Bunker dwellers. Twelve men. One trip. Zero self-control."

They all stood. Bottles clinked. Even the street vendors clapped. And as the sun finally dipped below the rooftops of Patong, and the market lights flickered on, casting everything in a soft golden glow, they raised their glasses one more time…. They sat back in satisfied silence — for a moment — until Pete clapped his hands and said,

"Right. Who's trying durian?"

Eleven heads turned. The air shifted. Somewhere in the distance, thunder rumbled. There it was: the King of Fruit, sitting on a wooden cart, spiky and ominous. A local vendor grinned like a man about to ruin someone's week and cracked it open. A wave of smell hit them like a punch to the throat. Imagine bin juice, armpit, burnt onion, cat vomit and betrayal — then add sugar. It was the olfactory equivalent of being mugged in a compost bin.

"Jesus Christ," said Steve, backing away. "Did something crawl inside and die while farting?"

Rory gagged instantly.

"Nope. That's a hate crime. My tongue just tried to leave my mouth."

Bernard sniffed it, blinked, and turned away.

"That's not food. That's a biohazard."

But Keith, wide-eyed and fearless, grabbed a chunk, popped it in his mouth, and chewed thoughtfully.

"Creamy," he said. "Almost… lovely."

Everyone stared at him like he'd grown another head.

Rory leaned in. "Mate, I don't know what you've been putting in your mouth this trip, but if you think that's nice, we need to have a chat."

Keith just shrugged. "Tastes like custard... with a side of bin."

They howled with laughter. Even the vendor laughed.

"Another one?" he asked hopefully.

"Twelve tequila shots instead," said Bruce. "And bring the bucket."

As the last of the durian funk drifted into the warm Phuket air, the boys raised their glasses one more time. The end was near. But the night was young. And Bangla was calling.

"To Bangla. One last tango," shouted Bruce

As the last durian bite was swallowed — or in most cases, spat violently into a napkin — the boys rose like a rogue tide and spilled back into the night. Beach Road shimmered under neon lights and the heavy, humid blanket of Phuket air. Scooters zipped past like mosquitoes on steroids. Music throbbed from every open bar. The sea, just across the road, glittered in the moonlight like it was winking at them. Then, like a man possessed by Bacardi and impulse, Craig suddenly took off running.

"Oi! Where's he going?" Steve shouted.

"He's cracked," said Pete, already jogging after him.

Craig, arms pumping, sprinted down the sandbank, kicked off his flip-flops mid-stride, and without breaking pace, dived headlong into the dark waves with the grace of a man who'd definitely done this before — but probably not sober.

He popped up with a yell:

"COME ON, YOU LOT!"

The rest didn't even hesitate. Screaming like teenagers, twelve half-pickled men bolted towards the sea, wallets in hats, shirts half off, shorts soaking fast. Bruce tripped over a sandcastle. Keith cannonballed like he thought it was the Olympics. Rory entered the water in slow motion, dramatically windmilling his arms for effect. The beach exploded with chaos.

Dripping and roaring, they gathered chest-deep in the warm surf, formed a lopsided circle, and began stomping through the water, arms around each other's shoulders, spinning slowly like drunken Druids at a beach rave.

Then Bruce shouted it — the chant that had followed them across three golf courses, seven bars, and one dodgy karaoke room.

"WE ARE YORKSHIRE!"

The circle erupted:

"WE ARE YORKSHIRE!" "WE ARE YORKSHIRE!"

Locals watched, bemused. A passing tourist filmed the whole thing. Somewhere, a crab decided to move beaches permanently. Splashing, spinning, shouting — these weren't just men on holiday. They were gladiators of midlife mayhem. They were legends of leisure. They were, for this one moment, immortal. And the sea didn't care who they were. But it carried their laughter out into the warm Phuket night like a final salute. Then, still dripping and howling, they turned as one and marched toward Bangla. It didn't matter that their clothes clung to them like damp tea towels. It didn't matter that their hair looked like a bunch of windswept garden hedges. It didn't even matter that Rory had apparently lost one flip-flop to the tide and was now barefoot and proud.

Songkran was still raging. Water guns fired from every angle, buckets flew from doorways, and the air smelled of jasmine, fried noodles, and recklessness. Girls in neon crop tops danced on bar counters, and tuk-tuks thumped with bass like mobile nightclubs.

"To the Koala!" someone yelled.

"Koala Bar or bust!"

They marched in, wet, loud, and laughing, like a crew of pirate survivors returning to the only port that ever understood them. The bar girls screamed in delight, arms open wide, as if welcoming home soldiers from war — or a dozen half-naked idiots with good bar tabs. Two buckets of beer landed on the table before they even sat down.

"Get these in ya, you legends!" Bruce shouted, wiping his face with a bar towel and immediately pouring himself a beer with the grace of a man who'd had twelve.

Keith was back with Trudy, who was feeding him shots like he was an injured bird. Pete was arm-wrestling a girl twice his size and losing with a big grin. Bernard had removed his shirt entirely, convinced it helped him dance better. And then, like a scene written in the stars...

Josh stood up.

"Josh… no…" muttered Steve, already laughing.

Josh turned, his eyes wild, water still dripping from his shorts.

"oh bloody well yes" he shouted as he rang the bell.

DING – DING – DING - DING!

The bar exploded.

The girls screamed. Music roared. A confetti cannon went off from somewhere no one could identify. A girl climbed on a table and tried to balance a tray of shots on her head.

Steve turned to Bruce and shouted over the chaos, "That's another 15,000 baht down the drain!"

Bruce clinked a beer with him and laughed.

"Best money we never spent!"

They hugged the girls, the staff, each other. Even Craig and Stu, now joint holders of the highly prestigious and entirely made-up Phuket Golf Champion title, raised a glass together in mutual respect. The Koala Bar — that glorious open-air madhouse — pulsed with their energy. For one final time, it was their home, their arena, their palace of poor decisions and unbeatable memories.

And as the night wore on, and the beers turned to buckets, and the crowd blurred into noise and neon, One thing was clear. This night wasn't over yet. Bruce, eyes blazing and sweat glistening on his forehead like a prize-fighter in round twelve, stood on a stool and raised his beer.

"Right, boys! Let's hit the next street. We need to drink this bloody road dry!"

Cheers erupted. Glasses slammed. High-fives flew. They spilled back into the street like a wet rugby team on the run from decency. Neon signs buzzed. Music poured from every open doorway. The smell of grilled squid, sweet chilli, and danger hung in the air like perfume.

They turned into the next alley; a glorious stretch of tiny open bars strung together like drunken dominoes. Pool tables leaned unevenly on tiled floors, girls leaned even more unevenly on tourists, and each bar had its own theme: cowboy, jungle, disco, and one that appeared to be entirely run by a family of cats in sunglasses.

"Let's play this game!" shouted Keith, pointing to a log with nails already hammered halfway in and a beaming girl standing nearby holding a wooden mallet like Thor on casual Friday.

The girl walked up, absolutely stunning — white shorts, blue crop top, a cheeky grin, and eyes that suggested she'd drunk lads like them for breakfast.

"Okay, boys," she purred. "Rules are simple. One nail. One hammer. One try per turn. First to get it flush wins. Ready?" "Born ready," said Keith, grabbing the mallet like it owed him money.

Whack! He nailed it. Dead centre. A clean hit. The nail sank halfway down.

"YEAHHHH!" the boys roared. Beers lifted. Bruce gave him a manly slap on the back that almost knocked the wind out of him.
The girl smirked.

"Watch this." With a flick of her wrist, she brought the hammer down with surgical precision — bang! The nail sat nearly flush.

"Ouch!" Keith winced. "You've done this before. What power! You hiding Thor's hammer down there?"

She winked. "You want to find out?"

"Oh, I'm not being beaten that easy," Keith grinned, puffed up and ready to reclaim his honour. He raised the mallet high, channelled every ounce of Chang and ego into his swing......and missed. The hammer missed the nail, smacked the log, and the mallet head exploded upward, twisting majestically through the humid night air like a poorly designed firework...CRACK! It landed squarely between John's eyes with the grace of a falling anvil.

"SHIIIIIIIT!" everyone shouted.

John stood motionless. Then swayed. Then sat straight down on the pavement like a pensioner who'd lost a game of musical chairs.
An egg-shaped bump erupted instantly, as if someone had inflated a balloon under his skin.

"Quick! Some ice!" the beautiful girl shouted, already halfway behind the bar. She returned, crouched in front of him and pressed the bag of ice to his forehead with unexpected tenderness.

"How's that feel, handsome?"

John winced. "Colder than Bruce's ex heart."

She smiled sweetly... and then, without missing a beat, grabbed him between the legs with her other hand.

"You need ice for this too?" she asked playfully.

John blinked, paused, then grinned.

"No love, just the head will do." The boys howled.

"Surely you can't be thinking of that now". Shouted Bruce. The beers sprayed. Someone fell off a stool. Even the DJ stopped the track to see what the hell just happened. John, ever the trooper, took a bow — well, a seated nod — and held the bag of ice like a medal of honour.

Keith? He was still arguing with the log.

"Rematch!" he shouted. "That bloody thing moved!" Keith shouted, still pointing accusingly at the innocent log like it had personally insulted his family.

The boys had barely stopped laughing from the mallet-to-the-face incident when Eric suddenly stood up, looking flushed and far too pleased with himself. He leaned over the bar, whispered something to the girl he'd been chatting up — a petite, dazzling vision with a dangerously flirtatious smile — then turned to the group.

"Right, lads! I'll be back soon. Just going for a... quick one for the road!"

"Bloody one for the road?" Bernie bellowed, raising his beer like a gavel. "It's 1 a.m.! That road's got potholes and regret all over it!"

The boys cheered him off like he was leaving for war. Eric disappeared into the neon-lit haze, hand-in-hand with his new flame. The rest of them? Right back to buckets of beer, cheap tequila shots, and singing off-key to whatever western pop hit the bar's sound system butchered next.

John, now with his mango-sized forehead lump proudly on display, posed for selfies with passing tourists. Forty-five minutes later, a dishevelled but euphoric Eric reappeared, stumbling into the bar like a cowboy returning from a gunfight — victorious, but clearly wounded.

"Eric!" Steve called out. "Where the hell have you been? You look like you've just done a triathlon in flip-flops!"

Then they saw it.

His right forearm was wrapped in cling film, shiny and taut like he'd gone into battle with a sandwich.

"Wait... what's this?" Bruce asked, narrowing his eyes.
Eric, eyes misty from Chang and choice, held up his arm like it was the Holy Grail. Underneath the cling film was a fresh tattoo.
In bold, slightly shaky script were the words:

"Cat above a love heart in bright red"

The ink still glistened. The skin around it was red and swollen, like it was already questioning its own life choices. There was a collective pause — then an explosion of laughter.

"You absolute bellend!" shouted Steve.

"Cat?! Who the hell's Cat?!" Pete asked between gasps for breath.

"The girl," Eric slurred proudly, "with the… you know… sparkly thing in her belly button. It's love."

"You met her like… an hour ago." said Rory, nearly crying with laughter.

Bruce staggered up, beer in one hand, phone in the other. "Mate, how are you explaining that to Bev when you get home?"

Eric blinked.

"Bev!" he said, like it was a name he'd heard once in a documentary. He grinned. "She won't mind. It's art."

"Yeah," said Craig. "So is the Mona Lisa, but you don't shag it and tattoo its name on your arm after three Bacardi's."

Bernie wiped tears from his eyes. "This trip. This bloody trip…" Someone started chanting, "Cat! Cat! Cat!" and within seconds, the whole bar joined in. Even the bartender held up a shot glass and shouted, "To cat"

Eric bowed drunkenly.

"She's got a sister, you know."

"Oh Christ," said Bruce. "Round two, incoming."

The cheer hadn't even died down when Steve appeared, arms draped tightly around Suki, the girl he'd now spent three nights with, and who'd become more possessive than a clingy house cat.

She looked flawless. Slender waist, elegant curves, dazzling smile — Steve was smitten. But there was no denying it: Suki wore the trousers. And possibly the belt, boots and matching whip. They walked up to the table like royalty entering a dive bar. Suki took the beer from Steve's hand and sipped it without asking. Steve looked at her like she was the northern star.

He leaned over to Bruce, eyes glazed but full of determination.

"I'm not coming home tomorrow with you guys."

Bruce paused mid-swig, slowly turned his head. "Eh?" He briefly wondered if Suki even knew his last name.

"I'm staying here," Steve said. "With Suki. We're together now."

Bruce's face contorted into the kind of confused horror usually reserved for tooth extractions and prostate exams.

"It's a holiday romance, you daft bugger!" Bruce hissed. "You've known her for what, three nights? That's not love — that's your nob talking to you. Get a grip!"

"I mean it," Steve said, eyes misting like he was giving a speech on Love Island. "I love Suki. She gets me."

Bruce looked at Suki, who was now texting someone on Steve's phone while finishing his beer. He turned back, deadpan.

"Mate… if you love her that much, bring her back to York. I'm sure Gloria will love her — the daughter she always dreamed of."

He started laughing, half-choking on his drink. "I mean it," Steve insisted, wobbling. "You can tell her for me. Please. Just tell her I'm happy."

Bruce shook his head, wide-eyed. "I'm not telling your mother you've fallen in love with someone you met over buckets and foot massages."

Steve leaned in closer, whispering like it was sacred. "We held hands in the market."

"Oh, bloody hell," Bruce muttered. "That's practically an engagement here."

Suki grabbed Steve by the collar and tugged him into a kiss that left no doubt who was steering this ship. Steve looked like he'd been tasered with passion. Bruce sighed and patted him on the shoulder.

"Alright, Romeo — we'll talk in the morning. The beer's talking now. And don't text your boss."

Steve nodded, totally unaware Suki had already added herself as an emergency contact in his phone.

Bruce turned to Pete and muttered, "I give it a week."

Pete shrugged. "I give it until breakfast."

The boys drank on, fuelled by equal parts nostalgia and whisky fumes, stumbling their way from bar to bar until they hit the final frontier — the infamous Indian nightclub on Bangla Road. It was one of those places where the floor vibrated with bass, the lights strobed like an alien abduction, and nobody could hear a damn thing but their own bad decisions echoing off the walls.

Strobe lights flashed. Cocktails flowed like waterfalls. Girls spun around poles like it was the Olympics. In the middle of it all was Steve, still glued to Suki, spinning together like a couple auditioning for Strictly Come Dancing: Drunken Edition. Steve was shirtless by now, for some reason. Suki had confiscated his wallet and was using it as a clutch bag. Nobody seemed to mind. Josh, ever the wildcard, came flying over the dancefloor, soaked in sweat, hair like a haystack of shame.

"Right lads!" he bellowed over the music. "I've only gone and booked us a bloody VIP table!"

The rest of them squinted at him like he'd just said he'd adopted a goat. Josh grinned, pointing toward the back of the club.

"Let's hit it — it's time to really get this party started!" It was the grin of a man who had definitely mistaken his overdraft limit for a challenge.

With that, the music paused for just a moment — the way it does when the club wants to show off. Then through the smoke and strobes, three stunning girls strutted in, hoisting drink trays aloft like Olympic torchbearers. Each tray had a bottle of Jack Daniels and towering sparklers fizzing like a fire hazard waiting to happen. The whole club turned and cheered as they approached the lads' table in slow motion, lights bouncing off the bottles like they were carrying the Holy Grail.

"Kin'ell Josh," said Bruce, shielding his eyes from the sparkler in front of his nose. "What did that cost?"

Josh just shrugged.

"Who cares, mate. Can't take it with me, can I?"

Bernard raised a toast: "To reckless spending and zero accountability!"

And with that, the JD and Coke flowed like a river in a storm. The table became a swirling mess of cackling laughter, drink-fuelled philosophies, and wildly inaccurate pool dancing. Craig was air-guitaring with a bar stool. Stu had his shirt on his head.

Pete was teaching a girl how to do the Macarena to house music.
Even Bernard, now wearing one of the sparkler sticks like a monocle, stood up on a chair to deliver a slurred speech about male bonding and gastrointestinal bravery.

Meanwhile, Steve and Suki were still orbiting each other like drunk satellites, spinning, dipping, laughing, kissing, and generally behaving like they'd already registered a joint bank account. And somehow, in all the madness, the night found a new gear. Because this wasn't just any send-off. This was the grand finale. The last chaotic, whisky-soaked salute to a week that would never be repeated — and frankly, probably shouldn't be.

Chapter Seventeen

Not a Cat in Hell's Chance

The room was spinning. Or maybe the fan was spinning, and Eric's brain was just trying to catch up. Either way, it was too bright, too loud, and his arm was absolutely throbbing.

His eyes squinted open, gluey with last night's sins. He felt something tight and plasticky against his skin and slowly turned his head to look.

There it was - His forearm. Still wrapped in cling film. Like a butcher's leftover. Like something you'd find in the back of the fridge and pray wasn't still edible. He peeled the film back like unwrapping a cursed relic... and there it was: A swollen, red heart. And inside it, in glorious permanent ink:

CAT Eric sat bolt upright.

"WHAT THE ACTUAL F—" he shouted to no one in particular.

He blinked at the ink. He shook his arm like maybe it would come off. He rubbed it furiously. He looked again.
Still there. Still CAT.

He staggered across the room like a wounded animal, half-tripping on a shoe, and grabbed his phone. Scrolled.
Found Bruce. Dialled.

Ringing – Ringing - Ringing—

"Hello…?" came a croaky, barely human voice on the other end.

"Bruce! It's me. Eric. Mate—I've done something really, really stupid."

Bruce groaned. "Mate. What time is it? What country am I in? My mouth tastes like death."

"I've got a f*ing tattoo, Bruce! **"

"Yep mate, I know. Not your smartest thing, have to say?"

"A fkin tattoo. On my arm. It says CAT. Like the animal. Like the girl from the bar last night. I don't even remember it happening, Bruce!" There was a pause.

Then Bruce wheezed a laugh. "Well, mate. Hope you like felines. Because you've adopted one for life."

"Bev is going to absolutely MURDER me. I was already border line, but thought I managed to save it over the phone. But now with this on my arm?! What do I say?!"

Bruce snorted. "Look on the bright side, she was probably going to kill you anyway for sneaking off, might as well be hung for a sheep as a lamb. Or in your case, a cat! Guess you could tell her you've always been fond of diggers!"

"This isn't funny, Bruce! I can't wear jumpers forever! It's Thailand! I'm SWEATING just thinking about it."

Bruce coughed. Possibly laughter. Possibly last night's tequila. "Well… let's look at the positives. At least it wasn't 'Ping Pong Girl' in gothic font."

"Don't. I'm already on Google trying to find laser removal in Leeds."

Bruce finally sat up in bed, fully enjoying the meltdown now.

"Look, you idiot. It's a holiday tattoo. You'll survive. Bev might not notice it if she's blindfolded for the next ten years."

"I need a plan. A story. Maybe I can say it's the initials of something meaningful."

"Like what? 'Can't Actually Think'? 'Completely And Totally plastered'?"

Eric groaned, there was a long silence. Then Bruce howled with laughter.

"You absolute melon. You're going to be the first man in Yorkshire to get kicked out of his house by someone named after a pet."

Eric looked again at the tattoo, now turning an angry shade of red.

"Not a CAT in hell's chance I'm getting away with this, let's meet downstairs in 5 and give it some thought."

Just as Eric was mid-spiral, sitting shirtless on the breakfast table, arm outstretched like it might fall off and looking like a man who'd just found out he was legally married to a houseplant, the door swung open.

In walked Bernie. Towel around his neck, sunglasses indoors, munching on a half-eaten banana like he was strolling into a scene from 1980s Miami Vice. He took one look at Eric's clingfilmed arm, clocked the swollen red tattoo, and instantly burst out laughing.

"Oh mate! You've only gone and branded yourself like a prize bull! CAT? What the hell were you thinking — was Garfield busy?" Eric didn't even have the energy to be offended.

"I don't know what happened, Bernie. One minute I'm doing shots, next minute I've got a bloody tribute to Whiskers the tabby on my arm. Bev's going to set me on fire."

Bernie wiped a tear from his eye as he chuckled, then suddenly stopped mid-chew.

"Wait... you know what, lad?" he said, his tone shifting from mocking to... vaguely inspired. "I actually have an idea."

Eric snapped upright like a meerkat on alert.

"Tell me. Please. Anything. I'll give you money. I'll name my next tattoo after you."

Bernie grinned, walking over and pointing at the monstrosity on Eric's arm.

"Right. So, you've got this CAT business already inked in, yeah? Fine. What you do now, is you get yourself down to that dodgy tattoo shop by the pharmacy— you know, the one where the bloke looks like he's on parole— and ask him to draw a cat. A proper one."

Eric blinked. "What kind of plan is that?!"

Bernie raised a finger. "A genius one. You tell Bev it's about your love of animals. Rescue cats. Childhood pet. Mental health therapy kitten. Pick one! You spin it right; you're not an idiot... you're a bleeding animal rights activist!"

Eric looked at him, dead serious. "Do you really think that'll work?"

Bernie shrugged, stuffing the rest of the banana in his mouth.

"Mate, we don't leave for the airport 'til 3pm. That gives you four hours and a lie so big it might just work."

He gave him a wink and started heading back out.

"Oh, and if it goes wrong… tell her it's short for 'Cathleen' — and that she died tragically in a bus crash. Instant sympathy."

Eric stood up abruptly, eyes wide. "That is actually fkin' BRILLIANT! **" he shouted, slapping his own forehead. "Why didn't I think of that?!"

He started pacing like a man possessed, arms waving wildly. "When we were first dating — Bev had this stupid little cat! What was its name… Katya! Katya the bloody rescue cat. Used to sit on her lap like it paid rent." He spun around, locking eyes with Bernie like he'd just seen the face of God.

"I'll tell her I was missing her so much, and thinking about those first sweet dates — that I got a tattoo of the cat. A tribute! An emotional bloody homage!"

He rushed across the room, grabbed Bernie by both ears, and kissed his forehead like he was the Pope.

"You're a fkin' genius, Bernard. You've saved my life. **"

Bernie grinned and shrugged.

"Well, I always thought I was. People don't listen, but I've got layers, me."

Before he could say another word, Eric was already halfway out the door, shirtless, hungover, and hellbent on commissioning the most heartfelt feline cover-up tattoo Southeast Asia had ever seen.

"Oi! Don't forget to tell him Katya was fluffy — none of that Sphynx cat shite!" Bernie shouted after him, chuckling as he sat on the edge of the bed. He looked over at Eric's half-empty bottle of water, picked it up, sniffed it, and winced.

"Vodka. Of course. Bloody animal."

Eric stumbled down the narrow Patong street, bleary-eyed, shirt half-buttoned, and hope clinging on by a thread. The clingfilm on his arm crackled with every panicked step. His mission was simple: turn a drunken disaster into a heartfelt tribute... to a cat. Eventually, he spotted the shop: Deadly Inking – Walk-ins Welcome, with a flickering neon skull above the door and a suspicious red stain on the step. Lovely.

He slumped into the sun-bleached plastic chair out front, sweat trickling down his back, still mildly drunk and now roasting in the morning heat. A few minutes later, the door creaked open and out walked a heavily inked Thai guy with a bandana, wraparound shades, and a beard that screamed retired roadie for Metallica. He jingled a huge keyring and nodded at Eric.

"You want finish tattoo?" he said in a deep gravelly voice, sliding open the metal shutter. Eric stood, bleary but determined.

"No, mate. I need a modification. Something more... personal."

He pulled out his phone, shakily scrolling until he found it — a grainy picture of a fluffy black-and-white cat lying on a tartan blanket.

"This. This is Katya My girlfriend's cat. She loved that thing. I'm gonna tell her this whole tattoo was for Katya."

The artist squinted at the phone and raised an eyebrow. "You want... cat?"

"Yeah. Full cat. Cute. Maybe some whiskers. Heart's already there, right?"

The guy scratched his chin, still staring at the photo. "Bro... I usually do skulls. Crossbones. Demon wings. Flaming serpent heads bursting out of eyeballs. No one's ever asked for a cat before."

Eric looked up, blinking. "Well, there's a first time for everything. Can you, do it?"

The man sighed, then slowly nodded.

"Yeah... why not. Let's make it cute. Sit down. Try not to cry."

Eric flopped into the chair and peeled off the clingfilm. The artist studied the drunken scrawl of "Cat" for a moment, then shook his head with a smirk.

"Romantic fool," he muttered, firing up the needle.

As the buzzing began and the outline of Katya took form, Eric winced and gritted his teeth. Halfway through, just as the guy was inking the cat's tail, the door banged loudly. THUMP. THUMP. THUMP. Eric twisted around in his chair. Outside, pressed against the glass like kids at a zoo, were the lads. Eleven of them. Sunburnt, hungover, and in full idiot mode.

Bruce was first.

"MEEE-OWWW!" he howled through cupped hands.
Pete mimed scratching at the window like a giant cat. Josh was doubled over laughing.

"Draw a little litter box next to it, Eric! Authentic touch!"
"Put a collar on it with Bev's name!" shouted Rory. "And a neutered tag!"

Eric gave them the finger without flinching. The needle buzzed on. Inside, the tattoo artist shook his head in disbelief. "Your friends... they are crazy."

"Tell me about it," Eric muttered through clenched teeth. Bruce called out, "Right, lads, Koala Bar! One for the road! Eric — don't catch rabies off that thing!"

The lot of them cackled like schoolboys and wandered off down the road, still meowing and shouting,
"We love you, Katya!"

The tattoo guy paused, hovering above the half-finished cat.

"You want... bow tie on it?"

Eric stared at the ceiling. "Sure. Why not. It's already mental." The man nodded solemnly. "Cool. First cat. Gonna put this one on Instagram, show my caring side!"

Eric arrived at the Koala Bar just as the afternoon heat began to settle into that sticky Phuket haze. His shirt was untucked, his sunglasses slightly wonky, and his entire right arm was wrapped in fresh clingfilm again — now with the majestic, wide-eyed face of Katya the Cat staring out through a slightly skewed love heart. He stepped into the familiar chaos of the open-air bar — the bass thumping, fans lazily spinning above, the smell of spilt tequila and coconut oil lingering in the air like a final memory.

The boys were already there, gathered around their usual spot — two buckets of Chang already sweating on the table, a tray of mystery shots lined up like liquid landmines, and a rotating cast of bar girls hanging on shoulders and giggling into the noise. As Eric slumped into the seat next to Bruce, he winced.

"Jesus Christ, it hurts like hell," he muttered, gently cradling his arm like it had just come out of surgery.

Bruce leaned over, raising an eyebrow at the plastic wrap. "Bloody cat tattoo, mate. You'll never live this down."

Eric groaned. "Tattoo hurts… my head hurts even more.

Pete raised his beer. "To Katya! Long may she purr!"

Everyone laughed as Eric flipped him the bird, then carefully pulled open the clingfilm just enough to show the others.

Rory squinted. "Looks like Garfield had a stroke."

Bernie chuckled. "Better than having 'Noi' tattooed across your heart. Now it's just confusing, not divorce-worthy."

Eric took a long swig from his Chang. "Let's just drink and never talk about this again."

The vibe was different now. The trip had reached that twilight point — the peak of the mountain had been hit, and they were on the slow, grinning descent.

The music still played, but a little softer. The drinks flowed, but a little slower. The girls were still laughing, but with the kind of affection you only get after seven nights of late-night flirting, endless tequila, and drunken declarations of true love.

Trudy sat next to Keith, twirling a rose from two nights ago. "You remember this, sexy man?"

Keith smiled. "Of course. That rose cost me a thousand baht and a permanent reminder of a cat named after sushi."

Suki, still draped over Steve, kissed him gently on the cheek. "You really not going back?"

Steve shrugged. "Not unless someone tackles me at check-in." Bruce raised his voice above the music. "Alright, lads — time to say your goodbyes."

One by one, they stood, hugs exchanged with the girls, kisses on cheeks, a few exchanged numbers that would go absolutely nowhere, and promises of returning that no one would really keep.

Josh rang the bell one last time — CLANG!
"Final round, boys!"
The girls cheered. Drinks came one more time. Toasts were made.

"To the caddies!"
"To Katya!"
"To that bloody mallet!"
"To Suki's dominatrix grip on Steve!"

The sun was now dropping behind the buildings, painting the street in gold. They all stood outside the Koala Bar for a moment, lined up like a bunch of misfit warriors. Arms around each other. Shirts untucked. Faces sweaty and grinning. A final group photo, blurry and perfect.

Then with a chorus of "see ya laters" and "don't forget your passports, you muppets," they turned, arms slung over shoulders, and began the walk back to the hotel.

The street behind them pulsed with music and laughter — but the chapter was closing. They had one last sleep ahead. One last night of being those lads again. And Eric, clutching his throbbing tattoo and his bag of mangoes from the night before, smiled to himself. At least Katya would live forever.

Chapter Eighteen

Will You Still Love Me, Tomorrow

Steve stood in the hazy Phuket afternoon outside the hotel, shirt half-buttoned, love-drunk eyes locked onto Suki's. She looked as glamorous and mysterious as ever, wearing sunglasses that cost more than Steve's flat-screen TV.

"I'm not coming back, lads," Steve declared, puffing his chest and holding Suki's hand like he'd just married a Thai Bond girl. "I've made my decision. Tell me mum, yeah? Tell her I've found happiness. Real happiness. Me and Suki… we're gonna build a future together."

The lads all exchanged slow, tired glances. Pete sipped a bottle of water. Eric scratched his tattoo through the clingfilm. Eric muttered,

"He's cracked. Fully lost it."

Bruce walked up slowly to Suki, pulled a crumpled wad of baht from his back pocket and handed it to her.

"For your troubles, love. We'll be in touch from Blighty."

"Okay ka," Suki replied, tucking the notes into her purse without breaking eye contact with Steve.

Then, in a blur of masculine intervention, twelve knackered Yorkshiremen hoisted Steve off the pavement like he was a rolled-up carpet and bundled him onto the waiting minibus. His limbs flailed, shouting "I love her!" as Suki waved serenely from the pavement. As the minibus pulled away, Bruce turned in his seat.

"She'll have a new Steve by sundown."

"Let's hope he's got a stronger liver," added Craig.

Phuket International Airport felt like a detox centre disguised as an air-conditioned building. It was too clean. Too quiet. Too... adult. Eric collapsed into a plastic chair by Gate 14, arm still throbbing from the freshly reworked "cat cover-up." The swelling now made it look like Garfield had been stung by a wasp. He winced.

"Hurts like hell. So does my head after that bloody mallet."

Bernie snorted, pulling out a mystery toastie from his bag.

"You're lucky, lad. That's not the worst thing that happened to your body this trip."

Across the lounge, Steve sat sulking with his sunglasses on indoors, sipping coconut water like it was a whisky sour. "She was the one, lads."

"Mate, she tucked that cash into her bag before you even hit the kerb," muttered Rory.

Craig, scrolling through his phone, added:

"She's already uploaded a new pic. She's with a Norwegian called Lars now."

Steve groaned.

Meanwhile, Bruce was struggling to zip his golf clubs into a travel bag clearly made for a budget yoga mat.

"Right," he grunted. "Who's got the bloody duct tape?"

The final boarding call rang out, and like hungover cattle, they shambled onto the plane. One by one, sunburned, sandal-wearing, and spiritually broken.

As the plane lifted into the sky, the tropical chaos of Thailand faded into a blur of clouds and regret. Keith turned to Rory.

"Back to the grind, mate. Council tax. Dog poo on the path. And Alan from accounts thinking he's hilarious."

Rory nodded solemnly. "Do you think I'll still fancy lager at home?"

"Nope." Chuckled Keith.

Meanwhile, Craig was trying to cram an industrial-sized Toblerone into the overhead locker while holding three cartons of duty-free fags under his arm like a budget octopus.

Bruce stood up once the seatbelt sign went off, arms wide like Moses with sunburn.

"Boys. It's been biblical. We drank. We danced. Some of us dry-humped on sunbeds. And despite Keith trying to seduce

street food vendors and John being KO'd by a flying mallet —
we survived. Yorkshire strong!"

A stewardess politely asked him to sit down. He gave her a
crisp salute with a half-eaten bag of onion rings. In the rows
behind, soft snores began, a choir of tired tigers dreaming of
sea breezes, tequila shots, and mystery bruises.

As the plane soared, twelve once-wild men floated toward the
inevitability of normal life. Back to emails. Back to thermostats
and laundry. Back to pretending the last ten days never
happened. And Steve?

He stared out the window, whispering, "Suki," like it was the
closing scene of a badly dubbed soap opera.

Back in economy row 28, Eric scratched his cat tattoo.

"Bloody Katya. You better be worth it."

Keith looked at his bag of mangoes with affection.

"Still smells like the beach."

And Bernie? He just laughed, shook his head and said,

"Right, whose round is it when we land in Dubai?"

The plane finally touched down in Dubai, the sun glaring bright through the windows as the tired, half-drunk lads stirred to life. Bags were grabbed, phones checked, and the slow shuffle toward the jet bridge began.

Josh, looking fresh as ever despite the chaos, turned to the boys with a grin. "Alright, lads, this is where I hop off. No messing about with duty free for me — straight to the exit for a taxi, then home."

Bruce slapped him hard on the back. "You're a legend, mate. A proper f**king legend. Thanks for being the best host and getting us this far."

Josh laughed. "Cheers, Bruce. Take care of yourselves, yeah? Don't do anything too stupid on the last leg."

Steve, still half-in-the-clouds, watched Josh walk away. His grin faded, replaced by a heavy sigh. He muttered, "I'm really going to miss Suki. Thought this was just a holiday fling, but… she's different, y'know?"

Bernie gave him a knowing look. "Aye, that's the way it sneaks up on you."

Eric rubbed the tattoo on his arm absentmindedly, then groaned. "Bev's going to kill me when she sees this. I mean, a big love heart and 'Cat' on my arm? She'll think I'm cheating or something."

Bruce shook his head with a smirk. "Mate, just tell her it's a tribute to Katya, her cat. You know, nostalgia and all that bollocks."

Eric laughed nervously. "Yeah, yeah, nostalgia… If only I had thought of that before the needle hit my skin."

Rory, sitting nearby, raised his water bottle.

"Well, at least it's not your name tattooed on a stranger's forehead. That would be commitment."

The guys chuckled, but the mood had shifted. The wild nights, the laughter, the reckless fun—they were all fading behind them. Steve shook his head, voice low but steady.

"Honestly, I don't want to think about going back to that empty flat. No Suki, no sun, just four walls."

Bernie patted him on the shoulder. "Mate, you'll be alright. Just remember this trip when it gets tough."

Eric sighed. "And I'll have some explaining to do about my new ink. I swear, Bev's going to think I lost my mind."

Bruce raised his bottle in a slow salute. "To us—brothers in arms, brothers on the green, and brothers who somehow made it through without too many broken bones."

They all lifted their bottles, some swaying slightly with the weight of their own emotions and the booze still coursing through their veins.

Josh, already halfway down the airport, looked back and shouted, "Until we ride again, boys! Keep the legend alive!"

The boys called back, "Safe flight, mate!" and "Don't be a stranger!" Josh disappeared into the terminal, no detours into duty free, no last-minute souvenir hunting—just straight home.

Steve closed his eyes, savouring the moment before reality hit again. Eric sighed, rubbing his arm and casting a glance at the tattoo now permanently part of his story.

Bruce grinned. "Alright, lads. One more leg to go. Let's make it count."

They moved forward together, the final chapter of their mad Thai adventure about to be written on the long flight home. As the plane began its slow descent toward Manchester, Bruce pressed his forehead to the cold glass of the window, peering down at the grey, soggy patchwork below.

"Look at that, Bernie. It's f**king raining. We've left paradise behind and landed in the most depressing place on the planet."

Bernie chuckled, shading his eyes from the glare of the cabin lights. "Could be worse, mate. Could be Heathrow, packed with all those bloody southerners. I'd rather face the rain than the traffic chaos and the hipsters."

Bruce laughed, the sound a little hollow but genuine. "True that. At least here, the rain feels honest. No pretending it's anything else."

Down below, the city spread out—wet pavements, soggy parks, people huddled under umbrellas rushing to get out of the miserable drizzle. Manchester in all its gloomy glory.

The boys shuffled in their seats, the buzz of the flight slowly wearing off as the reality of home crept in.

Finally, the wheels touched down with a splash, and the plane taxied toward the gate. The captain's voice crackled over the speakers,

"Welcome back to Manchester, everyone. Please remain seated until the seatbelt sign is turned off."

As they stood to disembark, the usual chorus of groans and laughter filled the cabin. The final moments of their wild adventure winding down. Once off the plane and moving through the airport's sterile halls, the boys made their way toward customs. The banter was light, the usual jabs and friendly punches exchanged as they tried to shake off the dullness of returning.

Suddenly, Steve's face fell as a customs officer stepped forward, motioning him aside.

Bruce's eyes widened. "Bernie, you didn't?"

Bernie shrugged, a mischievous grin spreading. "I bloody did."

Steve looked mortified but then cracked a half-smile as the rest burst out laughing.

"Oi, Steve, it's probably just because of the... eh, tattoo, mate," Bruce teased. "They probably think you're some kind of international art collector or something."

Steve rolled his eyes but was secretly relieved it wasn't something worse. As Steve went through the questioning, the others waited nearby, still chuckling.

Bernie nudged Bruce, "Well, at least you're not the one they picked. That was nearly me last time."

Bruce laughed, "Better you than me, mate."

The customs officer finally waved Steve through, and the group reunited, now fully back in reality but carrying the memories—and the stories—of a trip none of them would forget.

The bus rumbled out of Manchester, carrying the weary but wired lads northward to York. The chatter was a mix of laughter, yawns, and quiet reflections on the trip just ending. Outside, the English countryside blurred by — fields glistening under an overcast sky, the green far less vivid than the Thai sunsets they'd left behind.

As the bus pulled into York station, the group gathered their bags, stretching stiff limbs and blinking against the dull daylight. One by one, they shuffled down the steps and spilled onto the platform. There, gleaming black under the drizzly sky, sat Sasha's merc, idling patiently. Bernie wasted no time, grinning ear to ear as Sasha leaned out the window to greet him with an enthusiastic lick to the cheek. A few steps away,

Sandra and Bev stood waiting, arms crossed but smiles bright, scanning the crowd.

John nudged Eric, nodding toward the two women.

"Ok, mate. This looks positive," he said quietly, eyes glinting with encouragement.

Eric took a deep breath, feeling the lump in his throat, and they all walked toward the women.

"Did you have a great time?" Sandra asked, her voice warm, a gentle teasing tone for the others. The boys exchanged glances, laughing softly, all agreeing it was a trip to remember. With hugs and quick catch-ups, the group slowly parted ways — some heading home, some to cars, some simply wandering off into the familiar streets of York.

Later that evening, Eric sat quietly at home with Bev, the fading light casting soft shadows in the living room. He rolled up his sleeve, revealing the fresh tattoo — a neat black cat with a love heart beside it. Bev's eyes widened, then softened as Eric explained,

"It's a reminder of… well, of the start. Of Katya, the cat you used to have. I was thinking about our first dates, how much I missed you…"

Her eyes glistened with tears.

"You soppy sod," she whispered, reaching out to touch his arm. "I have missed you too. Fancy doing that and thinking of me."
She smiled through her tears. "I do love you, you know."

Eric pulled her close, feeling the warmth and weight of home — a different kind of paradise.

Steve's hand trembled slightly as he turned the key in the lock. The familiar click echoed through the quiet hallway. He pushed the door open and stepped inside, the comforting scent of home wrapping around him like a soft blanket.

From the kitchen came the sound of clinking dishes and soft humming. Gloria appeared, wiping her hands on a tea towel, her face lighting up as she spotted him.

"Steve! You're finally home," she smiled, crossing the room to pull him into a warm hug. "I've missed you."

He let out a breath he didn't know he'd been holding and hugged her back. "Missed you too." She stepped back and gestured toward the dining table, where a simple but hearty meal was laid out—roast chicken, steaming potatoes, and fresh vegetables.

"Dinner's ready. Your favourite," she said, pouring him a glass of wine.

Steve settled into his chair, the weight of the trip beginning to lift as he took in the familiar sights and smells. He looked around the cozy room, memories flooding back.

"You know," he began, voice a little rough, "I thought I could stay away forever, but… I've missed this. Missed home."

She smiled softly, sitting beside him. "We all have."

Later, as they cleared the table together, Steve grabbed the laundry basket with a grin. "Here comes the tourist's dirty laundry," he joked, tossing his worn clothes inside. Gloria laughed.

"Welcome back, love. You're home now."

A few streets away, Bruce trudged wearily toward his flat. The overcast sky matched his mood as a light drizzle began to fall. His hands buried deep in his pockets, he sighed, bracing himself for the quiet that awaited him.

But as he rounded the corner, he stopped in his tracks. Two small figures sat patiently on the doorstep—his kids, their faces lighting up the moment they spotted him.

"Dad!" they shouted together, leaping up and running toward him.

Bruce dropped his bag and scooped them into a big, warm hug. "You two been causing trouble without me?"

"We've missed you so much, Dad," his daughter whispered, clinging tight.

His son nodded eagerly. "Yeah, it's so good to have you back." Bruce's chest swelled with warmth, the weight of the trip melting away. Holding them close, he knew this was the true paradise.

"Come on, before you both freeze out here," he chuckled, unlocking the door and leading them inside to escape the damp York drizzle.

The following Saturday, the boys all arrived at their home turf—the familiar Emerald Pines Golf Club. The air was crisp, but the warmth between them was unmistakable as they greeted each other with hearty handshakes, pats on the back, and plenty of laughter. Memories from the trip poured out as they chatted, hilarious misadventures, close calls, and unexpected friendships.

Bruce made his way to the first tee, taking a moment to loosen up with a few deliberate practice swings. The others watched with a mixture of anticipation and amusement, knowing Bruce was up to something.

He paused, wiped a bead of rain from his brow, and turned to face the crew with a mischievous grin.

"Alright, lads. I've been thinking," he began, voice low but full of excitement. "Next year... Vietnam. Yeah, hear me out. The golf courses there are supposed to be something else—lush greens, stunning views. And as for the ladies..." He winked, causing a ripple of laughter to spread through the group.

"But, and it's a big but," Bruce held up a finger for dramatic effect, "we need to tread carefully. Last time, we might've been a bit... too enthusiastic with the drinks and the adventures. So, next trip, same fun—but maybe with just a little more finesse."

The boys nodded, some chuckling at the thought of a 'finessed' version of their trip.

"Anyway," Bruce continued, stepping up to tee the ball, "now watch this drive."

With a powerful swing, the ball exploded off the clubface, soaring clean and true down the fairway. "BOOOOOOM!" The shout rang out, echoing across the course. The others clapped and whooped, the spark of camaraderie as bright as ever. As the ball landed perfectly on the fairway, Bruce looked back at his mates, the gleam in his eyes promising the start of another unforgettable chapter. "Beat that if you can!"

Printed in Dunstable, United Kingdom